"HI MOMMA, IT'S ME"

"HI MOMMA, IT'S ME"

How Souls Stay Connected Forever and the Power of Undying Love

SANDY COWEN

Waterside Productions

Printed in the United States of America

First Printing, 2020

ISBN-13: 978-1-947637-06-1 print edition
ISBN-13: 978-1-941768-02-0 ebook edition

Waterside Productions

2055 Oxford Ave
Cardiff, CA 92007
www.waterside.com

To Charlie, Jack and Lucy,
the ones Jon loved the most

TABLE OF CONTENTS

INTRODUCTION

It's been many years since a fresh perspective on death and dying has been widely published and universally accepted. Still, we have learned as a society more about how to interact with our terminally ill loved ones and how to respect their wishes at the end. What's missing is knowledge about how to manage our own grief as well as accepting the reality of our own death.

To most of us the concept of death is frightening. The process of dying is a mystery and the thought of leaving those we love is sad and terrifying at the same time. The fact remains that this life experience carries with it a round-trip ticket; we just don't know the exact departure date. Intellectually people can probably grasp that fact, but on an emotional level accepting that one day we will simply vanish from existence is a tough pill to swallow.

What if, instead, we thought of death as merely a transition instead of a finale? A process by which our soul still remains nearby, and we are able to reconnect with those we love whenever we wish. Then, dying might not seem so final and eternal.

Hi Momma, It's Me is an account of a soul's struggle with the reality of death and the eventual joy that resulted after reuniting with the person who loved him the most, because she loved him the longest. This book is the story of a mother and son on a very special journey. It was written to remind us of the power of undying love, of how souls are connected forever, and as proof that a fascinating and glorious afterlife awaits.

As the author of this book and a person who has experienced many losses in life, I've never understood or felt the need to know much more about death than the obvious: it happens. Then, when my only child passed at 48, his death opened the door to a deeper understanding and more profound insights about the ultimate passage and what transpires after life.

The round-trip ticket theory became a startling reality when I found my son Jon's body. That moment left me stunned, but shortly after when I heard him call out his feelings of confusion and disbelief, we reconnected. From that moment forward, he and I started engaging in a new relationship that has become the most loving, richest relationship I have ever experienced, even when Jon was alive. This time we're connected soul-to-soul in total perfection, in limitless love and with complete understanding of each other.

Prior to Jon's departure, I knew nothing about the subject of death and dying. But there was a person who did, Dr. Elisabeth Kübler-Ross, MD, the major voice and pioneer in near-death studies. She was the author of the internationally bestselling book originally published in 1969, *On Death and Dying.* Dr. Kübler-Ross passed away in Scottsdale, Arizona in 2004 and I was fortunate to have met her more than once. She was a legend and her theory about the fives stages of grief was also known by professionals in medicine, psychiatry and the nonprofit world as the "Kübler-Ross model." As a psychiatrist and author, she brought dignity and self-respect to those near death. What many may not know is that this amazing woman was also an advocate for the existence of spiritual guides and the afterlife as well. She was open to additional possibilities that might exist.

I met Elisabeth Kübler-Ross through my dear friend Dr. Gladys McGarey, MD, MD(H), the "Mother of Holistic Medicine." Dr. Gladys was much more aware of the details of Elisabeth's work than I was, but I was still aware that Dr. Kübler-Ross was the inspiration behind the hospice movement and that she brought greater understanding to caring for dying patients than anyone else before or after.

The reason I interject Elisabeth Kübler-Ross into this book is that toward the end of her own life, she was known to remark to Dr. Gladys and others that her work was not the "last word" on the subject. She understood there was still more to know about the other side, the experience of passing and the afterlife.

I'm sure there will be many voices to help accomplish her wish. I just hope *Hi Momma, It's Me* is one of them. I wrote this book to shine a light on the passing of a soul, the soul's life after death, and to help explain what that process looks like. Is it scary? Is it peaceful? Where do we go and why do we go there? What are the lessons we learn? Why do we come into this life in the first place and are our loved ones lost forever, or is there a way to ever reconnect?

When I was called to write this account, I reached back to material I had stored away over many years. For decades I had been a reluctant medium, keeping this "gift" a secret from the public and maintaining detailed notes of each message I'd received from the other side. The notes were similar to the process of taking dictation. The information Jon was now sharing with me sounded eerily familiar to those received earlier. All the previous voices—family, friends, Ascended Masters and yes, even God— were all saying variations of the same thing over those many years. My son helped me lace all this incredible information together, along with his own insightful comments, to explain what transition is like, how Heaven works, and why it's important for souls to stay connected even after death. Primarily, he wanted to provide hope and open the doors so everyone could experience what he and I now have.

In reading *Hi Momma, It's Me,* I hope you'll suspend your skepticism and approach the subject with an open heart, not blindly accepting anything, but also willing to read through what is presented without totally dismissing it. Hopefully a couple of points will ring true for you, while a few others might make you think and perhaps others will engage your compassionate side. Mainly, I hope this book will help people heal their sorrow and grief and find a greater gift within their loss.

It's fitting that I completed the writing of this book on Easter Sunday, a day that celebrates Jesus' resurrection from death. There's a parallel here with the resurrection and reunification that occurred then and to the reconnecting between souls we can experience now. I hope this parallel will make sense to you as you read on. The thought that all of us can be reunited with our departed loved ones again while we still remain on this earth isn't just a fantasy. As you will see, it could very easily happen.

Chapter 1

"MOMMA, I DON'T KNOW WHAT HAPPENED"

The most painful experience in the world is being helpless in the face of your child's suffering. In this case, my child was forty-eight years old, but had left this earth a few hours before. As I sat in a chair in the next room, the medical examiner and police were in with my son. I wasn't alone in the family room—a police officer and a counselor were with me too. Sitting still, most likely in shock, I heard my son. The voice in my head was crystal clear. I knew he was no longer in the room, which had been temporarily his, but wherever he was he was talking to me.

I heard his confusion, his fear and his sorrow. I felt bits of what he felt and what I was hearing and feeling magnified the shock of my loss. I felt what he felt: the fear, the horrible sadness and regret. There was no doubt all of this was real because I had dealt with many other souls over the last twenty-eight years that were confused about transitioning to the other side too. I knew this was a struggle my son's soul was facing as he tried to move on to peace and, finally, to Heaven.

Hearing what Jon was going through, even in short clipped messages, left me feeling helpless and desperate to help, but I could not. My pain was overwhelming since I had just lost the one person closer to me than anyone in the world: my only child, the love of my life, my son.

Jon was living with me at the time, and when he failed to go to work that Monday morning, I went to see why. It was July 2, 2018 at 8:30 AM when I knocked on his door. His car was out front so I knew he was home but it was so unusual for him to still be here at that time of day. So, I knocked again. Nothing. On the other side of the door, it felt eerily quiet, unnatural. I opened the door just a bit and as I did, I called louder to him.

"Honey, are you awake? Jon, are you up?"

Then, as the door opened slightly wider, I saw his arm raised in bed and he was lying on his side with his face hidden by the pillow next to him. Instantly, I knew something was very wrong. The thought that went through my mind as I reached out to touch his arm was *Oh, no*. When I touched him, he was cold. I think he had been gone for hours.

"You left."

I barely managed to utter. It was like I knew he had a choice. You see, from the time my son was born and I saw his adorable little face sticking out from the tight swaddling that enveloped him, I had a different attitude than most parents do about this birth and this child.

Nearly fifty years ago, doctors didn't do things the way they do today. I wasn't given my baby to hold immediately after his delivery, perhaps because I had passed out briefly. They weren't that great with pain-free deliveries then either. So, while I was waking up, they cleaned and wrapped my baby, then woke me. They asked if I wanted to see my son. I turned my head and there he was. He was beautiful, wide-eyed and curious lying in an incubator-type transport they used at that time to move newborns into the nursery. He was simply amazing. But I knew he wasn't mine, he was merely a gift for me to love and care for until he grew up and had a life of his own. Still, in that instant, my heart overflowed.

I had wanted a child for years and was married for four years before a pregnancy finally stuck. In those days, again, most of my friends by age twenty-five already had a young family— one, two or even three little ones. There I was, still wishing. Finally, at age twenty-four, I became pregnant and the next year Jon was born. I named him Jonathan, which meant "gift of the Lord."

You know how some people are very possessive about their children and believe they are "theirs"? They talk about "their blood" and become all fanatic about their offspring. I never felt any of that. I somehow knew each human has a soul and each soul is different from one another, even those related. Later I learned that each soul has its own journey and each of us has a choice about when we come back. I was given Jon for a reason and I was to be part of his story and journey on this earth. I was honored but never felt like I owned him.

I was a loving mother, a strict disciplinarian, and tried to foster joy in my son's life. I offered guidance, but like all kids, by the time Jon was a teen all that advice just ricocheted off his head. I could almost see it start to enter into one ear and then bounce right off him every time I offered an opinion. Jon was his own person.

Now, my son was gone. When the police and medical examiner arrived, they had insisted on doing whatever they did with Jon privately and asked that I move into another room. That's where I was when I heard my son asking for help. Throughout the day, I heard him a couple more times. I didn't write down what he said but his words were burned into my memory. It would be easy to transcribe them later.

My son had died. He screwed up and was gone. He didn't mean to do it, it was an accident, but he was reckless and now his life was over. I knew this was an accident because Jon never would have intentionally left his three beautiful children, whom he adored, nor would he have wanted me to find him. As proof, Jon had texted me the day before his death with a photo of his daughter, Lucy, and her friend on the beach. He asked: "Sometime in the next 4-6 months either for b-day or X-mas can you blow up Lucy's face so it's just her and frame it for me?? Love this shot of her, don't you??" Then, the very morning of his death he seemed to be in the middle of a big deal at work and had sent a text to a client at 2:35 AM about papers he would drop off to him later that very day. Yep. This was definitely some deadly mistake.

What led to Jon's passing is a long story, but one that is important to be shared, not only so you can understand the context of all the messages that follow, but because his life illustrates the horrible consequences of addiction and why it's so dangerous to purchase any drug on the street instead of relying on a doctor's prescription.

As the police were checking Jon's possessions in the room where he had been living, they found a vile of pills that appeared to be street drugs: oxycodone, specifically. And these professionals were sure the pills had been laced with fentanyl, a deadly drug that is fifty to a hundred times stronger than heroin. They guessed that the oxycodone mixed with fentanyl had likely killed my son instantly. Jon didn't know what hit him.

Jon never would have planned such an ending. This was a massive screwup. He had been needlessly reckless and his death was the tragic result. That was confirmed by what I heard him say throughout that day. There was no question that he wasn't ready for what eventually happened.

Specifically, these are the messages I heard as my baby boy's soul struggled to understand what had happened to him:

> *"Oh, Momma. I don't know what happened. I'm so sorry. I'm so sorry"*

Then, after a brief pause, Jon continued:

> *"I didn't mean for this to happen."*

It was heartbreaking to hear these words come into my head, as I sat there completely blank. He said slightly after.

> *"I don't want to leave,"*

I tried to comfort him and let him know that he had passed, that his life had ended and that it would be okay. I asked him if he could see a light or anything, and to go toward that. I was trying to help him find peace.

> *"I will Momma, I'm trying,"*

But, I could still feel his fear and confusion.

> *"Momma, I'm scared."*

I fell apart. It was hard enough to realize my son was gone and that I'd never see him again. But now to also feel the pain of his transition was almost too much for me.

It was horrible to bear witness to the agonizing emotional distress a person sometimes feels after death: being afraid and not wanting to leave. I think when it's a complete surprise that shock and confusion are more likely to occur, even on the soul level. And there I was, witnessing Jon's struggle, unable to help the one person I loved more than anyone else in this world.

The Path to Addiction

The story surrounding Jon's addiction was equally tragic. Two years before, my son had come to live with me while he was getting on his feet from an unfortunate series of events. Those events began when he became financially overcommitted from a divorce nine years prior and not being able to climb out from under the debt. The settlement and subsequent alimony Jon had agreed to in negotiating the divorce from his former wife and the mother of his three children, was mainly based on the value of the commercial real estate business he had started just a year or so before. The settlement was large, but it was fair since Arizona is a community-property state.

Unfortunately one-year after the settlement and twelve months of substantial payments, the economy was still in the midst of the horrible recession that began around 2008. Jon's company was beginning to suffer as a result too. Once worth a million or more, Jon's commercial real estate business was now worth nothing. Jon struggled to maintain his business, keep his people employed and pay this personal debt. But, the retail sector of the commercial real estate business was particularly hard hit during that recession and, as we can all remember, that recession lasted for years and years.

Because his company was now worth nothing, Jon could have returned to court and renegotiated the settlement to some amount more realistic, but he didn't. He wanted to remain the provider, the hero to his family, and he wanted to take care of his former wife and children without question. After a couple of years, a large regional commercial firm acquired his company to start their retail division, but by then Jon's clients were practically inactive, his income was pretty slim and the employees he managed to save became more of a burden to the new company than a gift. I think Jon's payout in the acquisition was something like $100,000 – only ten percent of the million dollars his former company was worth. So, maintaining payments to his ex-wife on the nearly $500,000 settlement was impossible now. Still, Jon hung in there without renegotiating the debt. Noble thought but poor judgment.

Jon had put himself under a lot of pressure trying to do the right thing. But, that pressure seemed to exacerbate an issue that had also been in play all along. I believe my son had been a very high-functioning alcoholic for a number of years. He didn't binge drink and he didn't drink all the time, but he drank a lot when he decided to seriously party. That had been his history but nobody seemed to comment much about it. Jon was charming, funny and his drinking never interfered with his home or work life. In fact, Jon was a good time and lots of fun when he drank and in commercial real estate being a lot of fun was more of an asset than a liability.

The negative effects of this budding addiction over time grew more apparent, and soon some of his friends and I began to recognize that his judgment was waning. Not renegotiating the divorce settlement was one example, but once in a while socially his excessing drinking and the need to have another drink, led him to take personal risks that weren't physically dangerous but would eventually be damaging to his reputation.

Still, with all the pressure Jon was facing, he was really well-liked. Jon was the eternal optimist and a charismatic salesman. That one more big deal on the horizon was always there for Jon, regardless of the reality of the market. In hindsight, he probably would have been better off switching to another facet of commercial real estate during that period, but he stayed in retail. This was, again, not a wise choice for someone who needed a sizable monthly income, but it was the path Jon was on. Perhaps that was another sign his judgment was not perfect.

There is one other issue that had plagued Jon for some time; continual back pain.

Eventually the constant pain led to one back surgery, and a couple years later another. After the first surgery, I can remember picking Jon up from the surgery center where the doctors had written a prescription for ninety Vicodin tablets or maybe it was oxycodone or OxyContin pills, but whichever it was, the strength of each was 10 mg. Those pain pills at half the strength would have been addictive after five days, but with Jon's preexisting addictive personality and drinking history, this was a bad situation waiting to happen. I was ignorant then, as was Jon, and we didn't understand the impact of all of this and how soon he would become hooked.

With the first prescription, maybe Jon only needed to take twenty or thirty of the Vicodin tablets in total, but he took all ninety over time. By the time of his second back surgery and multiple prescriptions later, Jon's addiction had grown to twenty pills a day. He was sleeping constantly, made it into the office infrequently, and his lack of focus on work eventually destroyed his relationship with his clients and ended the relationship with his employer.

The one saving grace at this point was, because of Jon's extraordinary personality and the personal friendships he had established over the years, he had developed some amazing friends within the industry. It was those friends who did an intervention, arranged for everything and hauled him off to rehab. My son called me on the way there to tell me that it was the happiest day of his life. He was about to get clean and sober, to start his life over and he couldn't wait for it all to begin. Jon was completely sincere.

It's a long story about how he came back, found a new employer in the same field and began to rebuild his career. And in a commission-only industry, that was a tough slog with financial obligations the size of Jon's. I won't go into too much detail except to say that he was really trying to make it work and climb out from under the mountain of debt. That debt had continued to increase while he was in detox and recovery for several months, with no income. Now the hole he was in was even deeper.

What is important to share is how Jon came to live with me. That occurred when he was released from jail. Yes, unable to catch up on the payments as quickly as was expected, the judge threw him in jail until he could pay some $11,000 in back alimony to his former wife. That was obviously a surprise to Jon, who showed up in court with no attorney since he couldn't afford one, hoping to negotiate new terms. So, when they hauled Jon off to jail, the job he had recently acquired vanished and during that period he also ended up losing his apartment. His vehicle was also towed off the street to some impound lot.

First they took Jon to the county jail and then he was transferred to another jail. After several weeks he was finally allowed a work furlough and was housed in "tent city," Sheriff Joe's famous facility in Phoenix. This was in the summer when the temperature was over 100 degrees. All the inmates stayed in large tents. Many, who were kept in those secured tents, were on a work permit program whereby they could leave jail at 8 AM for work each weekday but had to report back by 5 PM each evening.

During this time Jon was trying to find a new job and someone to loan him money to be released. Meanwhile, he was beginning to look dreadful with a beard that had grown out, his hair was longer and he was losing weight; this was not a dress-for-success scenario. Thank God many in the industry knew him from before.

Then, because of Jon's talent and amazing group of friends, a former employer from years before, Marty DeRito, hired him back, loaned him the back support payments and put him on a small draw. Marty DeRito is a saint. With that incredible gift, Jon began for the second time to rebuild his career while he remained in the retail sector of the commercial real estate industry.

When my son was finally released from being incarcerated, I was in the parking lot waiting for him. As he walked to my car, I saw someone I barely recognized. Jon was disheveled, wearing the dress slacks and white shirt he had worn when he was taken to jail, they were now wrinkled and didn't fit since he was much thinner. With the longer hair and unkempt beard, my approaching son broke my heart. Still, I could see the spark that was always in his eyes. My son was somewhere inside that tragic looking man.

I took Jon to breakfast and since he had no apartment and no money, I told him he could stay with me until he got on his feet. Frankly, it was the best two years of my life because I got to see my son every day. I did his laundry, ironed his shirts and bought the groceries while he started his new position. Jon was still clean and sober; it had been three years to that point.

I'm shortcutting this story and will explain the relevant details later, but right now what's important is what happened in the two years that followed. Although Jon had been in the program (AA) for those three prior years, for some reason he had begun pulling away prior to his death. Jon went out the night before he died at 8:30 PM. He rarely left the house in the evening like that, but he came into my room and told me not to be concerned if I heard the door later that night. He was just going out for a while. I didn't worry and fell soundly asleep.

The next morning was July 2, 2018. It was the worst day of my life.

Chapter 2
OUR DIALOGUE CONTINUES

I may have been in some degree of shock for a couple months but people said I still handled everything amazingly well—from basic interaction to all the prep work needed for Jon's service and reception. Like many of you know, life doesn't completely stop—even with such a loss—and living alone, I still had to function day-to-day.

I managed to produce a video for Jon's service and in the process had to select some 120 photos from my more than seventy photo albums, picked the music and oversaw the editing. The video turned out perfectly. Staying busy helped.

Jon's service was beautiful, too. It was a Catholic Mass at the Franciscan Renewal Center in Paradise Valley, Arizona. They had just built a beautiful new church, which held 600. Jon's service was on July 17, 2018 in the middle of the hot Arizona summer, and the place was packed. There were people standing in the back unable to find seats. It was also unusual at that time of year to see most of the men in slacks, dress shirts and jackets; many wearing bow ties, Jon's signature attire. Jon's two sons, Charlie and Jack, wore his ties and Lucy, his only daughter, appeared with one of his ties on her wrist. It was a very touching tribute but not surprising from such thoughtful children.

Jon's reception was equally impressive. One of his industry friends insisted on paying for most everything connected with the service and another paid for the reception at the Arizona Country Club. Probably 300 or so attended the reception which followed. One of my friends donated the flowers, another handled the photography and helped me the night before set up displays for the reception. Jon's service and

Celebration of Life was truly beautiful and a fitting tribute for his children to witness.

Jon's send-off was amazing regardless of the fact that he was not a perfect person because none of us are. He was, however, a perfect friend and a devoted father and his personality, charm and sense of humor lifted everyone around him. He had a generous heart and seemed to light up any room he entered. I guess that was evident by the extremely large number of people who came to pay their respects, and to those, to this day, who still stay in touch with me.

I established an educational trust at a local bank to benefit Jon's children's higher education in lieu of flowers. My grandchildren were 12, 17 and 18 at the time and it was important that Jon make this kind of contribution to their futures since he had no assets to leave them when he passed.

The Secret

Although I was able to cope over those final days, I was keeping a secret from most everyone. I had been hearing from my son throughout this time. Fact is, had it not been for Jon's connection with me, I'd have still been in bed after the second or third day of his passing. Jon continued to reach out to comfort me and try to make me feel better.

Let me back up a bit to the third day after his death. I shared that Jon's confusion and fear had really been devastating for me to bear on top of the shock of his loss. But on the third morning, I was waking up When I heard a knock on my bedroom door. A real knock. Since no one lived in the house except me, there weren't many options. I knew it was Jon. I was half asleep and my eyes were shut. I thought this was probably just some type of imaginary experience, but regardless, I didn't want it to end. I clenched my eyes tight so the aberration, or whatever it was, wouldn't disappear. Somehow I knew this experience was something real; still, my conscious mind wasn't sure. With my eyes closed tightly, I could still see in my mind's eye Jon's form move into my bedroom. It was not clearly defined, but I knew it was my son. He turned to his left and sat in the chair where he had always sat when he came to talk.

Jon was emotionless, looked stunned or confused and said he didn't know what to do. He wasn't sure what had happened and was coming to me for help or advice or something. We talked for about twenty minutes. The dialogue went back and forth and always with my eyes clenched tight for fear I'd lose him again. I told him he had passed on and that now it was time to let go and move on to Heaven. He had no idea what that meant. I am sure my son was still in shock.

Then I did a corny thing and told him about a light to look for. Even if he only saw a glimmer, I told him to totally let go and surrender to that light. I tried to explain everything that would be waiting for him on the other side. The light, I explained, was the signal for the best direction for him to go. Everything else would come easily after that.

The way I'm explaining this is not specifically what I said, since I really don't remember my exact words. But given the fact that I had transitioned probably 1,500 spirits which were stuck over the last twenty-eight years, this process was not terribly new to me. But, this was clearly the most important transition I had ever facilitated. I was honored that my son had come to me for help with something so sacred. I was honored that when it was most important, he came to his mom.

At the end of our chat, I'm not sure if he had understood everything I was saying to him, but before long, Jon faded away. I hoped he had heard me, but regardless, I had done the best I could. That evening I felt completely at peace; for the first time since he had died, I was no longer worried. I knew my son was home.

On July 5, 2019, I heard from Jon once again. I asked if it was him, and like he would always say from that point forward, *"Yes, Momma."* Momma is what he always called me. I ran to my desk, grabbed a pen and tablet and wrote everything I heard. I wrote and wrote and wrote. This first message ended up being five full pages on a lined yellow pad. The following is part of what my son said on the first visit when I could actually transcribe every word.

"I'm with God now. You were right all along. Love is wonderful.
I'm happy and not sure what to call it—bliss or what—but wanted

to tell you how much I love you and to watch over Charlie, Jack and Lucy for me.

"I'm so very sorry. I was selfish and stupid and I guess not strong enough to deal with these addiction issues. Please forgive me Momma. I never would have ever hurt you like this and please let the kids know I love them more than anything I can express; kind of like it feels up here.

"Yes, I came to you in the bedroom, and yes, I reached out to you twice or more before. I didn't know what happened. I made a mistake—a big mistake. I guess I made a lot of those in my life, but more than anything I want you to know not to worry about me anymore. I'm here now and I'm safe."

Jon wrote much more to me in that note, but not everything is appropriate to appear in this book. I can tell you this, however, over the last two years I have continued to hear from my son. When he comes to me, I write it all down because I could never remember the humor, the brilliant insight he shares or the messages he wants me to give others. Then I go back and read what he said. It's more or less like taking dictation. It comes so very fast that sometimes I have to ask him to slow down so I can catch up. And, my son is a talker so it's pages and pages and I love every word.

I will quote throughout this book bits and pieces of the dozens and dozens of messages I've received. I receive at least three a month, I'd guess. Some of those messages are communicated to help us all understand what the other side is really like, some so he could explain his life and journey more fully to me and so it might help others, and some to express his love to those he cares deeply about, especially his children. Still other messages simply assuage his guilt. I'll explain a little later why relieving guilt is so important for those who pass. Right now, it's enough to know that we all have guilt we carry needlessly. Some for things we said and did in our lives, and some for the things we neglected to do.

Unburdening our souls is part of the healing experience, regardless of where we are. It's more difficult to unburden ourselves of guilt all by ourselves, and much easier to do if we can actually communicate with the person we've harmed. That's one of the ways our souls grow, and since spiritual growth is a never-ending process, it doesn't stop just because we've moved to another dimension. So, even over there, souls frequently try to connect with us to say they're sorry to the people they loved and harmed during their life. The only sad part of this process is that most of us who remain behind are not open to receiving those messages.

Some of the messages those on the other side try to communicate to us are often very short and simple like "I love you," I'm okay" or "I'm sorry." Generally it's the basics. But, sometimes these souls want us to know more. When we're open to them, it's possible to gain extraordinary insight about a child or parent we thought we knew, develop a better understanding of our loved one's journey and sometimes gain insight about our own lives.

Our Communication Begins

Jon's humor comes through in his messages to me generally in a word or two, but I typically either laugh out loud or a broad smile crosses my face. That isn't much of a surprise since when Jon was alive he had a wonderful sense of humor too. He was sincerely funny. At his Celebration of Life, many friends shared stories to illustrate experiences they had shared with Jon and how my son made them laugh.

One of my favorites came from the wife of one of Jon's dearest, lifelong friends, who came up to me to share a story about the first time she had met Jon. It was on that day, she said, when she fell in love with my son (figuratively speaking). Her name is Tammy. Tammy's intended was Chris, who was Jon's friend since Little League. Chris met his wife-to-be in LA, I believe, and she was in law enforcement too. Some special division, I think, but regardless she was a full-fledged police person with impressive credentials, as I remember. Anyway, Chris brought his wife-to-be back to Arizona and was taking her to the apartment he was sharing with Jon and another lifelong friend to introduce her to his buddies. The two roomies were at the apartment when Chris walked in with his future bride. The moment Jon saw this pretty blonde he threw his arms against the wall, spread his legs, and said, "frisk me." Everyone immediately broke into laughter and that's when Tammy decided she was crazy about my son.

Jon's quick wit was irresistible. However, with his mother, Jon wasn't afraid to show his other side. As an adult, he often treated me the same way he did when he was a teenager—which was not particularly attractive from a forty-year-old. Jon wouldn't hesitate to roll his eyes and make faces when I would bring up something he didn't want to hear about. Favorite topics for such a reaction were alternative medicine, my spiritual work or anything else that was truly unconventional. He thought I was "woo-woo." Maybe I was, but that was a side of my life that I rarely discussed, even with those who knew me. That was private and I treated everything I had experienced or was learning in that arena with a great deal of respect. Not so my son.

Ironically when Jon found himself on the other side, things changed. Amazingly, it was a snap for him to take advantage of the gifts I had developed. Our new communication process is now so normal, and that's why Jon now reminds me that he was always spiritual, which I do not doubt because of his innate kindness and compassion. But, I guess his life just got in the way of those gifts ever surfacing.

In one message, I shared with him how amazed I was at his perceptiveness and reflectiveness so soon after passing. In this particular note, it had only been a few days. So, I asked how he could possibly process everything so quickly. It seemed astounding to me. My son very quickly responded:

"Momma, I was always enlightened. I was just numbed to those gifts my whole life with the alcohol—then pills. I could have been like you.☺"

I was curious because he seemed so wise and insightful even though he'd been gone for such a short time. I had assumed that process would require a lot of self – reflection, soul-searching (excuse the pun) and the like. So, I asked him about that too.

"Not as much as you think. I'm in the accelerated course. Mary Grace [Warner], MD, MD(H), was right. Karma stuff—but all is good now that that's over. I know you always worried about me but that is over now too. Relax. Have a life. You are the most remarkable woman I have ever known and I am so proud you were my mother."

First off, my heart filled with pride for that validation from my son who had been critical of me for so long about many, many things. But, his karma comment is what stuck with me. I couldn't wait to hear more about that because I understand the concept of karma and have some idea about how it works, but have never heard a real life example explained to me, especially from someone who had lived it. So, I had hoped Jon would explain his experience with karma when he was ready.

To clarify, Mary Grace Warner, MD, MD(H) is my homeopath and good friend. She was a gifted integrative cardiologist, the first in Arizona a number of years ago, and later in her career she transitioned to homeopathy. She is enlightened herself and I think that serves her well in this new field. I see her every few months, and when Jon left she mentioned that his life this time was a Karmic experience. I sort of brushed it off, thinking maybe that was just an offhanded comment. Nope, she was spot-on.

When Jon finally wanted to talk about his life and personal karma experience, it came nineteen days after he had left. I asked him specifically about that and this is what he said:

"I can tell you, in past lives I was judgmental. Thought I was 'hot shit', looked down on others, had no empathy or compassion for their struggles."

He went on to explain how this time around he had to learn what it felt like to not be able to do anything right and to be helpless to fix his own life. Also, ironically, although I was the one person he would have been wisest to listen to, he wasn't able to do that because it would have interfered with his lesson and his journey this time. Then, Jon continued.

"You were always right. But my life this time was to learn what it feels like and how powerless it is to be a total fuckup! However, my heart was good, I tried and did have a pretty funny sense of humor, so all was not lost."

Because I want this book to be authentic in every respect, I apologize for not editing out the bad language, but Jon was expressive and I'm sharing exactly what he communicated with me.

Life and life's lessons are so fascinating, and it's smart to remember that we can never truly judge another. We do enough of that for ourselves when we arrive at the end of our life. So, in assessing others' lives, we can't possibly know what lessons they are to learn, what karma they must endure or what they may be teaching us just by being in our lives in the first place. All that comes much more in focus on the other side.

A More Pure Relationship

The one huge takeaway from the messages from Jon over the first month was that our relationship is now totally pure again, just like the relationship we had when he was a little guy. From the time he was a toddler until he was about seven years old, Jon was like a little angel; people could feel pure love pouring out of him. He was full of grace and maybe that's the way he came here, but I also think part of his love-saturation level had to do with the fact that I adored him so and kissed his face off until he was three or four.

Jon lived surrounded by love and I believe he was also an open channel for God's love. When love fills up a person who is pure like that, it just spills out onto everyone that person meets. People sense it right away and love to be around such joy. Even as an adult, with all of his issues and failings, I think some people sensed the light that still emanated from dear Jon.

Anyway, I know this story might sound like I'm exaggerating, but at age five Jon was enrolled in a very expensive day school called Phoenix Country Day School (PCDS). As a single mom at the time, I wanted highly capable people not only teaching but also carefully monitoring my son, although it took nearly half of my earnings to do so. I needed to know there were people near him who could let me know if Jon was showing any signs of needing more than what I was able to give him. His father and I were divorced and he wasn't really around when Jon was young. PCDS was the additional insurance I needed that my son was okay.

Well, Jon was a compassionate, caring little guy and made a big impression on his teachers. For example, if a little kid fell down in the schoolyard, Jon was the first one to comfort that youngster and to help. In fact, two of Jon's teachers, I believe for kindergarten and first grade, both cried at the parent/teacher conference I attended. Well, they got dewy-eyed as they both gushed over how sweet and what a wonderful little boy Jon was. I heard more than once from a teacher that if she ever had a little boy, she'd want him to be just like my son. In fact, I can remember being a little embarrassed at how effusive his teachers were about how kind and loving Jon was.

Going back further, when Jon was a toddler and people would come to our house, he'd be so excited to see them that he'd hug and lay his head on their leg in the most grateful and loving fashion. Jon pretty much glowed. Our relationship together was pure and loving and wonderful too.

Then my son grew up and, like all preteens and teenagers, he became his own person with the good and the bad. Throughout the rest of Jon's life, he was shaped by the development of his personality, societal pressures, and his own personal fears, many of which came as a surprise to me. He was afraid of dogs, for example. No idea where that came from since he was never exposed to dogs that I knew of and we had none at home. Other life-shaping factors were recognizing his own weaknesses, his reactions to the positive and negative experiences he faced routinely and the ebbing and flowing of emotions that faced any teenage boy.

I can remember the summer before Jon turned eighteen. He was five foot eight and probably weighed 120 pounds soaking wet. Sitting on the edge of his bed, he told me he would not go to the beach in California again until he had hair on his legs. Jon was a late bloomer. He eventually grew to six-two and 175 pounds. Still, Jon's teenage years were laced with insecurities and helped shape the man he would later become. Without a buff teenage body, he developed a stronger personality and other skills. He was never vain; he was caring. He wasn't girl-crazy; he was a best friend.

When I remarried and Jon was about five by then, he became very close to his new stepfather, and was influenced by him. That was initially okay with me since Jon needed a man in his life. But Jon's stepfather, Steve, wasn't the ideal role model. In private, Steve eventually became emotionally abusive to me and I discovered was a very high-functioning alcoholic. When the three of us were together, he was Jon's best friend and I was the outsider. His influence contributed to Jon pulling further away from me over the years. I guess the bonding was a boy thing.

But his stepfather also had some anger issues and was not the greatest communicator, so soon I began to notice disrespect and insecurities surface from Jon too. He rarely asked for advice (except on clothes once in a while) and began living the path he was destined for. Some of this process was painful for me to watch, but regardless of whether we were close or not, I knew somewhere deep inside that my son loved me very much. Just knowing that and the fact that Jon was somewhere near, geographically, I could handle whatever came. I adored my son.

The last two years of his life were more of a bridge of reconnection for the two of us than anything else. Jon was more tolerant, more loving and more respectful. That may have been colored by his gratitude because I took him in, but I actually think he was finally getting to know me as an adult, and not through the eyes of a man still emotionally fifteen years of age. I believe Jon's early drinking stunted his emotional development and influenced our relationship for decades.

Passing to the other side stripped Jon of all life's baggage: the physical struggles, the emotional issues, the weaknesses, the frustrations and other experiences that shape behavior. In moving to the other side, Jon became pure again. That same sweet, loving soul was now all that remained; he glowed so brightly when he first arrived and continued to do so until he began donning the garments of life that we all drag around with us. Now on the other side, nothing was left to hide the beauty of Jon's soul.

My son had become the same "light" given to me when he was born. Love flows unconditionally through him again, and our communication is, once more, honest and sincere and there is no baggage of any kind to get in the way. It is absolutely the same as it was when he was an innocent little boy. It is totally pure.

Profound Wisdom with Personality

The lighthearted way Jon answers many of the questions I ask is refreshing. He doesn't make things mysterious or too deep. He simplifies everything, explains clearly and delivers it all with a touch of humor.

For example, I asked him about someone else who had recently passed. A friend of mine, Marlene, had a very special mother who passed away a month after Jon. The mother was ninety-six, I believe. Mar had been incredibly supportive during Jon's funeral. She helped set everything up at the reception site and took amazing photos throughout, even though her mother was quite ill. Shortly before I received another message from Jon, I had attended Marlene's mom's funeral.

Marlene's mother was a wonderful woman. Morene smiled all the time, had an angelic presence and was generous and kind. She loved Jesus and was a devout Christian. I went to see her when she was near passing. She was in bed, but when I walked in Morene's face lit up because I think she just loved everyone and was grateful someone had come to visit. She passed a few days later.

In reflection, Mar told me that she would come into her mother's room and Morene would be smiling.

"What are you smiling at Mom?"

Mar would ask and her mother would respond, without hesitation:

"Jesus,"

Morene was ready to go and made her transition peacefully, and I believe she flew into Jesus's arms.

Her recent passing and the eagerness with which she embraced death contrasted with the struggle and confusion Jon faced. That dichotomy prompted me to ask Jonathan whether all people ascended into Heaven at the same rate, remembering that it had taken him about three days of turmoil and confusion to make his way to his final destination. Jon knew I was referring to Mar's mother since he and I had discussed her funeral a minute or two prior.

"No," Jon said. *"Marlene's mom took the express elevator. She just zipped up here. She was ready. She had been talking to the Lord and she was pure. I, on the other hand, had no idea what was happening to me and was in shock. It took some time to get my bearings (three days to be exact) and that is probably the average. Then, I got to where I needed to be. Some never make it, 'cause they don't feel worthy, don't believe, and all the other things you know from transitioning spirits. Your information on all of that is correct."*

More on my own experience transitioning souls and what I learned from that later.

However, when I shared the "express elevator" story with Marlene, she laughed.

Marlene is a very Christian woman as well, and would never delve into the occult or anything that was dark or mysterious. However, she knew me well and knew my heart was pure, that I was living in light, was close to God and knew Jesus too. So ever since then, she always asks me about what I've heard from Jon, and once or twice has mentioned to me that she wishes she could also have the same relationship with her mom.

Realizing that this kind of connection is possible is the first step for anyone to survive the death of someone they cherish. Realizing those we lost are really not far away is the second step, and that our loved ones' souls actually do watch over us and try to communicate, also helps. That awareness and later realization, hopefully, will make their grief more bearable.

I hope in subsequent chapters I'll be able to peel away the layers of this onion so the truth about how close our loved ones really are can be known and understood. In the process, we'll also find that regardless of who your child or spouse or friend ended up being in life, the beauty and love you initially saw in that person is now the only thing that remains. Once a person passes on, they become as pure and amazing as you remember them to have been—perhaps even more so. And, any bad feelings or anger they may have directed toward you or others no longer exists; it totally disappears.

I have a friend who shared, when I said I was writing this book, that her mother had passed some years before and that she had been an absolutely horrid mother. They were estranged for decades before the mother's death.

"Well," I responded, "I'll bet she feels immeasurable regret now, in fact, there is no question that she is very, very sorry. That's just how it works." So, if my friend could become open to recognizing signals or signs of connection, I'll bet she'd hear her mother say, "I'm so sorry."

Hate, anger, resentment and all the other negative emotions we express in this life cannot exist in an environment of pure love. That is what Heaven appears to be, as you'll read about in later chapters. Souls on the other side are enveloped in pure love. That's all there is over there. It's amazing how God's unconditional love heals everything.

But before we go much further, let me share a little about my backstory and whether we need to be afraid of this "connection" phenomenon or not.

Chapter 3

SOME RELIGION AND LOTS OF SPIRITUALITY

I suppose this is a good time to provide a little history about my personal spiritual path and how I've been able to, on one hand have a close relationship with God and be led by the Holy Spirit daily, and on the other hand still do work across dimensions. Well, I believe that anyone can take advantage of God's extraordinary gifts while remaining devoted and spiritual.

I was born Roman Catholic but can remember when I made my first Communion, standing in front of Visitation Catholic School in Kewanee, Illinois waiting with the other kids to walk to church as a group, thinking that somehow I didn't belong there. Something didn't ring true for me. I don't know why I thought that the Church and I were disconnected, but it was a powerful memory and occurred when I was about eight years of age.

I immediately pushed that thinking out of my head and went on to be a dutiful Catholic girl, through my early marriage at eighteen and up until my divorce at twenty. It was then I realized that the Church didn't want me anymore, as a divorced woman, so I simply faded away from Catholicism. That was in 1964.

By 1965 I had met and married a Jewish man who was quite a bit older than me, sixteen years to be exact. Bobby was a confirmed bachelor from Beverly Hills and I fell in love with this very unconventional, newly transplanted Phoenician. Bobby was also not much of a Jew. He hadn't had a Bar Mitzvah, didn't attend temple—even on High Holy Days, and his parents weren't terribly religious either. All of his family were Reform Jews and only went to services on Yom Kippur and Rosh Hashanah. When we were in LA, Bobby and I went with them and I felt comfortable at services. Maybe it was because I always found my place in the book before anyone else. The matriarchal culture of Judaism felt right to me and I felt like I belonged. So, later I converted. My conversion was a big surprise to Bobby.

I didn't convert as a Reform Jew, which probably wouldn't have taken as long, but rather as a Conservative Jew, with the most observant Jews being the Orthodox. Now, I'm not sure this was a hundred-percent complete conversion since right before my mikvah, or holy bath—similar to a baptism, Rabbi Moshe Tutnauer, my teacher, moved to Jerusalem. So I guess I ended up being a ninety-percent Jew.

I wasn't terribly observant either but I did study a lot prior to the conversion and attended High Holidays occasionally at Temple Beth Israel. I wore the mantle of Judaism proudly, always wore a Star of David around my neck and gravitated toward Jewish friends. I really felt at home for the first time in my life. Even though that religious discipline for me eventually faded, after Bobby and I were divorced, there was no doubt my heart was always and still is with the Jewish people. If nothing else, I'm an adopted Jew.

"The Girls" and Spirituality

By the late 70's I was remarried again and now not practicing any religion. Ten years later, I developed a friendship with a woman who turned out to be my closest friend. She had been the senior vice president of the largest local utility, and introduced me to a couple of other women she liked very much. One was a national political research professional from Washington, DC, who had recently moved to Arizona and another was a psychologist who coached executives. The latter had moved from Seattle with her husband not many years prior. The four of us represented Judaism, Catholicism, Christian Science and Latter Day Saints (LDS or Mormon). We were quite a group. We travelled together and explored our spirituality—meaning the gifts we believed God had given to us. We discussed all facets of life and human potential. We prayed together on occasion, and although we never spoke of our original religious teachings and none of us were still practicing our religions of origins we were always respectful of all religions.

In the past, I had read about and experienced many religions. In my advertising and public relations life, having owned a full-service agency for more than twenty-five years in Arizona, one of my clients was an author who'd studied with many great religious leaders around the world. Reading his book and meeting with him, over time, provided additional insight.

My dearest friend of these three traveling "sisters" was Shirley, the utility executive. She soon brought Michael Murphy, cofounder of the Esalen Institute in California and an early leader of the Human Potential Movement, to her company to conduct workshops. He taught company executives to be more mindful and focused in their daily work. A couple of us were invited to attend those workshops too. The sessions were directed toward meditation, or clearing the mind, but Shirley relabeled that exercise "concentration" for easier acceptance in the corporate world.

I could go on and on about what the four of us explored and learned about ourselves over several years, but as I said before, it was always God-centered. Since that time, although the other three returned to their original religions, I did not. I decided that a direct connection with God was the most rewarding for me.

One of the four of us, Cathy, became quite connected to the hierarchy of the Jesus Christ of Latter Day Saints Church in Salt Lake, after we drifted apart. She was a single woman but quite devout in her later years. I asked her once about her religion, and she said that upon death a woman had to be invited into the Kingdom of Heaven by a man. I don't remember the exact words but it sounded like the husband ushers his wife into Heaven and if a woman is single, another man is appointed to do that for her. Again, I don't remember the exact context but I do remember that, because Cathy was still single, I was concerned for her.

So, after Cathy died from leukemia, she came to me as I was driving in my car. Her visit came not more than a week after she had passed. I could feel her there just like she was right next to me. I asked her if she had to have some man invite her into Heaven. Her reply was sweet but very candid:

"No. That wasn't true, but they meant well."

That pretty much sums up organized religion to me. The purity of worshiping God gets gummed up in all the rituals, conditions, rules and add-ons that men or groups of men interject when constructing the religious process. So much of it that has nothing to do with a direct relationship with the Almighty. It's as if their egos make it necessary to complicate things—an add-on here and an add-on there. Pretty soon the group that was designing a horse ends up with a camel. I don't think that is what God originally intended for any of His children to endure.

A year or so later Cathy came to me again, this time at home. I was thankful because now I could transcribe everything she said precisely. This time, about religion, she said:

"Religion is odd. Men do screw it up. Starts out pure and then egos, intellect and peer pressure distort the purity."

Cathy's philosophy about life, in general, was lovely so I thought I'd insert the next quote in here even though it has nothing to do with religion; it just fit with the kind of person Cathy was:

"You have it right. Total surrender to life, to God, to guidance. Like floating down the Verde River on an inner tube. A little bumpy once in a while, but a fun ride if we share it with friends. That's what God wants for us. To enjoy the ride, laugh with friends, help one another and if our bottoms get a little cold and our tops get a little sunburned, what the heck! That's life."

Cathy was a dear friend and I wish she'd have reached out to me when she was so ill with leukemia. I could have helped her but that wasn't to be, so now I stay friends with her from another place. What Cathy shared is the way I try to live. Being appreciative daily of every gift around me, enjoying my friendships, having as much fun as possible while honoring God. I talk to Him daily, the Holy Spirit guides me in all I do and I pledge each morning to do His work faithfully. I merely ask to be led to serve.

Death Awakens Deeper Connections

The exception to my avoidance of formal religion is when Jon died, I did jump back to Catholicism, which still holds a place in my heart. I made my first confession, or as the Catholic Church now calls it "Reconciliation," in fifty-five years. I was able to do that since my first husband, when I was married in the Church, had since passed away. So I was able to take Communion at Jon's funeral mass, which I wanted very much to do. I still respect the Church and attend once in a while with my grandchildren.

Now I straddle both worlds, I guess, totally respectful of all religion and yet personally not needing the guidance of others or the fellowship of other worshipers near me to feel His presence. All I need daily is the one-on-one connection with Him to guide my life.

I've also come to know many realities of life and the life beyond this one through learning that has occurred totally outside of the world of religion. Yet for me, they seem to blend. The Lord seems to bless my work and makes it very easy for me to grow daily in all of these areas. It's therefore difficult for me to imagine that any of the gifts I've developed over the years, or my ability to cross dimensions in conversation, is anything but blessed by the Lord. It is also not surprising to me that people I know who are deeply religious still honor my gifts and don't seem to shun me or think I'm odd when I speak about Jon and still being connected to him. Some don't press it further, some ask questions and some are definitely curious—but none of them think I'm the devil.

A Spiritual Gift and How it Works

There is no question to me that what I do today is because of a spiritual gift. I also believe anyone could develop this same gift but that most people are either fearful of it, deny it exists or are closed off to growth, in any form. That makes me sad because much of humanity misses the richness available to them in the total life experience.

Being fearful and denying are pretty clear explanations of why this gift eludes so many, but being closed off is a description that may require a bit further explanation. You may have heard the expression that it's impossible to receive with a closed fist. In other words, one's hands must be open to receive; a clenched fist won't work for that. It's the same with one's heart. The kind of work I do is not possible with a closed heart. Since it's all heart-based there can be no judgment. One must remain loving with an open heart and a heart that's eager to receive.

Over the years, I assumed this was a gift God gave us all. So once in a quiet space, I asked. God speaks to my heart through the Holy Sprit, but a handful of times over the last thirty years He has come to me in more direct and complete messages. This was a bit of both. When I asked if this connectedness was a specific gift from Him that all of us could access, to be clear and to receive from the other side as I do, this was what I heard in response:

> "To be clear is your choice. No gift there. To receive is my gift to all: my voice, the Holy Spirit, my sons and daughters, teachers and Masters—Jesus, of course. Buddha and other departed souls—all voices in love, are my gift to you."

I understood immediately that He meant the channel was His gift, so the messages could flow from those with Him on the other side. However, to receive such a gift is a choice we make —if we are willing to become clear enough mentally and to receive without fear. To make this easier, let me explain "clear."

One's mind has to remain quiet. It's impossible to become a channel or receptor for communication that might flow to us if a person's mind is continually active and spinning with the day-to-day. One has to have a clear mind to receive. That's why meditation is a healthy exercise. In other words, practicing pushing away "busy" stuff that continually floats into our minds every second of the day.

Learning how to meditate teaches all to stay more grounded and to live in the present moment, to quit projecting into the future causing worry and stress, and to stop living in the past which can foster guilt, regret and sadness. The present moment is God's gift to us. That is when we appreciate fully the joys of life, the beauty of nature and the power of love. However, once we have mastered living in the moment, one still has to keep one's mind less busy so we are free to receive. One doesn't have to be in a state of meditation to receive a signal or to see a sign that we are being contacted, but once that happens then the mind must be totally clear to receive the message purely.

I feel blessed that I've learned that discipline, am not judgmental about the amazing abilities we all possess and have managed to keep this particular gift special. I've kept this gift free from commercialism or the potential to be influenced by dark or negative energy. Meaning, if I have ever helped anyone connect with those they love, I've never solicited any type of remuneration for doing so. I also have never tried to build a reputation for this service, never encouraged others to call me about doing more of this, and in fact have resigned most of my work in this arena to a very private place, away from public scrutiny.

To give you an idea of how I have used this gift to help others, when Jon died I reached out the next day to a man I had dated briefly a year or so prior. He was a successful entrepreneur, now retired, and a cowboy. He had the most common sense of almost anyone I had ever known (must have been the cowboy in him) and he too had lost a son. He knew the pain I was facing, so during the first couple of days he was a big help to me. Our history is interesting.

Months prior while we were dating, I had told him that I connected with those on the other side from time to time, thinking he'd run for the woods. Instead, he asked me if I could possibly contact his son. Now, Rod is a religious man, as well. Not sure which religion, maybe he is Catholic or Episcopalian, but anyway, he had insight into me, knew my heart and knew I wouldn't exaggerate my abilities, and in fact, if anything knew I would probably minimize them. He wanted my help. Unfortunately, I had to inform him that I didn't solicit souls to communicate with me.

"I don't reach out to ask for people to come to me, I believe that process just opens the door for mischief from those who may not be pure or true. Instead, what I suggest, is that when you're talking to your son, which I'm sure you probably do from time to time, simply tell him that you have a friend named Sandy and if he wants to communicate with you, he can do so through me." I continued, "It's up to those on the other side to initiate any type of a link with me as I don't interfere with connections that are this sacred."

My friend understood and said he would do just that. A few days later, I was walking into the back bedroom for something and an image appeared in my mind along with a single word. I just knew it was Rod's son. So I reached for a paper and pen and began to write. I will not share any of this with you since it is very private, but I called Rod, read him the message and then mailed the copy off to him. He had no doubt this was the son he adored and the message brought him a great deal of comfort.

I know what I do is blessed because what I receive is always warm, loving and comforting. No one profits from it. I didn't offer to do this work nor did I instigate the communication with someone on the other side. Further, I didn't tell others about it or use it to promote myself in anyway. I keep this part of my life sacred.

My friend asked for help, deeply loved his son and I merely facilitated that connection. Jon's messages are the same way. He comes to me with what he wants to say. He generally comforts me and showers me with a great deal of love in the process. He is a bit like my cheerleader some-times, since it is difficult being alone and not having any real support at this stage of my life. Once in a while he asks me for help with something, generally having to do with his children, and I do my best to accommodate. That's the give and take. That is passing love back and forth and that is helping one another.

Now, I am not a student of the Bible, but I know that one of God's most simple and basic teachings is that we are to love one another and help each other. Even if you are an agnostic or atheist, common sense tells us that appears to be the right thing to do.

I also don't believe that anywhere in the Bible God says that our love or the support of one another has only to be in horizontal relationships. Of course we love those passed but who says they can't or don't love us back? We may pray for those who have departed but who says they can't try to help us too? Who says that dynamic couldn't occur vertically across dimensions, as well as horizontally with our family, friends and acquaintances?

Another dear friend of mine named Paige chatted with me the other day on the phone about what I always say about the vertical and the horizontal. Paige is also someone who is quite gifted herself and said,

"You know what that is, don't you?"

I was just blank but she responded quickly.

"A cross,".

I immediately thought, of course, life is really very simple, isn't it?

If someday we find there are beings from another galaxy or universe that we encounter, I would imagine we'd want that same dynamic to occur: to be able to help one another and have love for one another in the process. So, limiting all relationships to just the people we know on earth seems silly to me and given what I know now, it's not realistic at all.

Every time Jon reaches out, this becomes more evident to me, and frankly, it has been apparent every time others who have passed have reached out to me too. Sometimes those on the other side aren't looking for anything from me, but sometimes they are.

Chapter 4
THE RELUCTANT MEDIUM

Prior to 1981, I was just the typical Type A personality, going at full speed, overworked, overstressed and overcommitted. One day my body broke down from eight years of taxing myself to the limit with so many stressors that it would require a whole other book to explain. In fact, I did write a whole other book about those experiences and my three decades of recovering, naturally, from chronic and critical illnesses. The book I wrote in 2008 was titled *Get Well: Even When You've Been Told You Can't.* That book focused on healing holistically and how that process works.

No need to go into any of that now, except to say, if it wasn't for the illnesses I faced throughout my life, I never would have slowed down long enough to develop the gifts God has given me, and us all. Instead, most people live like gerbils in a cage, like I did, and miss the richest parts of this life experience. Gerbils, you see, are not very loving or enlightened like other pets are; dogs and cats immediately come to mind—well, not so much cats. Gerbils, however, are different. Those little guys just keep running and running and running until they drop dead or their wheel breaks. Thank goodness my wheel broke. My body gave out and when I became ill, I was given the time to recognize and grab onto one of the best gifts I have ever received in my life.

I was just thirty-seven years old at the time when the first of my auto-immune conditions hit with a vengeance. That illness was rheumatoid arthritis (RA), a chronic inflammatory disorder that affects the joints. It's a very painful, crippling, disfiguring and degenerative disease. My attacks were random, extraordinarily painful and lasted for days at a time.

Now, again, without digressing too far off the point of this book, I'll try to describe why my healing journey may have been unique. I tried conventional medicine for my RA only long enough to realize that my condition really wasn't getting better instead my meds were getting stronger. I wanted complete healing, so I was committed to do no more damage to my body than it had already endured. Therefore, I looked for alternative options instead of the toxic chemicals that were being prescribed for this condition by conventional medicine. I took no pharmaceuticals and my journey to wellness became a bit of a trial and error process.

The alternative route was painful to initiate since I took no anti-inflammatory drugs and sought to reboot my immune system naturally so it would quit attacking me and return to normal. That process took a couple years. Meanwhile, to relieve the pain, I experimented with various supplements and learned that keeping my mind quiet had very powerful benefits. Quieting the mind, I found, made my pain less intense. Conversely, when my mind was racing the painful throbbing got worse, especially toward evening. As a result, I learned to make my mind still and only later did I realize that what I'd been doing had a name: meditation. For me, quieting the mind had become an instinctive process that helped.

Quick note: In Michael Murphy's meditation class that my friend Shirley had facilitated at the utility company where she was employed, I realized what I had been doing for years prior was actually called meditation. I was shocked, and frankly proud of myself that I had mastered something most people struggle to master.

In the several years that followed, whenever a mild attack or threat of RA occurred, I was instantly reminded to keep my mind totally quiet, or blank. In fact, I became so disciplined at this habit that my mind remained blank most of the time. This was not a "blonde thing"; it was a discipline I had mastered.

In fact, I once attended a self-help workshop that dealt with journaling and the workshop leader kept saying how important it was to rid our minds of all the clutter we store up there. He stressed that journaling would help us do that. So, we were instructed to pick a time of day that was comfortable for us, grab a note pad or journal and then write down whatever came into our minds. We were to journal the free flow of consciousness which filled our minds. I tried that but found when I sat down to write, nothing happened. I was so used to gently pushing thoughts away automatically that I guess random thoughts just eventually gave up. I couldn't write what didn't appear. I still tried and tried and soon, instead of eliminating the thoughts, that for most people were ever-present, I started receiving. Those other forms of information were interesting.

This time the thoughts weren't the lyrics to songs, worries about the future or thoughts about the past; they were filled with advice, guidance and comforting messages from somewhere else. Initially I had no idea where those bits of information were coming from, if they were valid or even if I needed to pay attention to them. Still, they weren't messages I could put aside; they were brief, to the point and sometimes weren't words but images—and were always of value.

I also didn't have to sit with a pen in my hand and a notepad in front of me to be contacted. Messages came, whenever. Sometimes they weren't even words—it was like my body was telling me things to do too. For instance, while I was walking through the house, my head would turn automatically and then I'd see something I needed to take to the meeting I was leaving for in an hour. It was like my body was saying, "Hey you. Look over there." It got to the point where I began to say, "Thank you." Or, if I was in a meeting, a point I needed to make would pop into my head. When I was out and about, an errand I had yet to take care of would also flash into my mind like a gentle nudge. We all get similar messages all the time but rarely pay attention to them. I, however, was attentive to all of it. Sometimes I would hear "be patient" or "don't worry." So, my first experiences with receiving were random and scattered, but eventually they would all lead to becoming a channel and then a medium.

Some of these messages may have come from the Holy Spirit as guidance but at that point in my life I could not connect those dots. I just accepted the gifts, wherever they originated, and kept on with my life.

Let's now explore the channeling part. Channeling messages from the other side did not come to me quickly nor was it even a goal of mine.

Everything in my entire sphere of experiences has more or less been accidental. In taking first things first, initially I learned that there was something that existed on the other side and it could reach me. I also learned these dimensions were a reality. Most importantly, I realized I was not afraid of it at all.

The Ghost Buster Myth

My first awareness of other, real dimensions came when I was confronted with my first ghost. Actually, this spirit was a soul who couldn't transition to where she was supposed to be. She was stuck. That space wasn't purgatory, as I was taught in Sunday school, it was just the dimension between where I was and where she were supposed to go—Heaven, to us.

The awareness of all this unraveled some thirty years ago when I was married to Jon's stepfather, Steve. We had been married perhaps ten years and had moved into a beautiful, historic home built in 1927 in North Phoenix.

Over the first couple years we lived there, I'd been told that a spirit also inhabited our residence. Actually, two different psychics who told me that at separate times, and each unsolicited. I could have cared less. I didn't even mention it to my husband, who probably wouldn't have believed it anyway.

But, Steve was a very sensitive Pisces. He was also the first one of us to meet our spirit, face-to-face, one evening in the solarium of our home. He later told me about his experience and related that he named the spirit Florence. He also gave her a job; if she was going to hang around she'd protect our home from harm. Who knows if that worked, but Steve was a pretty practical man. The whole idea of a spirit hanging around was interesting but I didn't jump into all the drama around any of it, and frankly neither did Steve. Between us, it was just a matter-of-fact.

Several months later, there were three of us at our home for a totally different reason and the subject of Florence presented itself. We were all in the solarium where Steve had actually encountered Florence. My friend Shirley was there as well as her friend, Stephan, an amazing healer who was working on me that afternoon. While we were chatting away, my husband walked into the house and ended up in the same room. That was unusual for Steve since he rarely came in when I had guests during the day.

Anyway, for some reason Florence became part of the discussion. We talked about how Steve had seen this woman in a dress with fringe and a feather in her hair—or rather an image of her, but not totally clear. Some might have thought Florence was a Native American woman because of the fringe and the feather, but what flashed in my mind was something totally different. So I asked Steve if the feather pointed straight up or outward in a curve. Steve said the latter. Florence was a flapper and the dress was a light fabric with silky fringe, not leather fringe, as many would have initially guessed. At this point I figured Florence had been gone for probably four or five decades.

As the three of us chatted about this soul, my husband was simply standing in the doorway of the room when someone asked,

"I wonder why Florence is still hanging around?"

I was the one to quickly reply and what I said even startled me.

"I think she's just too attached to material things."

Those words flew out of my mouth, and I had no idea why. Then, in an instant, all four of us had immediate, dramatic but totally different emotional reactions to what happened next. Steve's shirt, within seconds, was completely soaked from front to back. I started to tear up. Stephan got chills and Shirley heard a shrill piercing sound much like that made by a defective hearing aid. We all felt these powerful but extraordinarily different reactions at the exact same moment. At the same time, we all felt the energy in the room lighten and knew that Florence was gone.

We were stunned initially and then Shirley ran outside and looked up at the sky. When she did, she said our house had a sort of glow around it. She also heard, coming from somewhere:

"Thank you. Thank you. Thank you,"

Florence was free and that was the first of many unusual and fascinating experiences that I encountered over the next several years. Although other witnesses were present, I was the one who released Florence but still had no idea why I said what I said. Those words just came automatically.

Over the next two or three years many more souls, who were stuck, came to me. I used to joke that there was probably a neon sign over my house that said "This way up." When praying about why this was happening to me, I was told that Archangel Michael was bringing me these poor souls because I was loving, open, not fearful of the process and nonjudgmental. Over time, I realized that transitioning from this life to the next for a few souls can be a real challenge, and generally, it is how messed up we are in this life that gets in the way.

All in all I've helped transition some 1,500 souls, some of whom came in small groups, to the afterlife. I'm most grateful for this experience, but the experience only lasted three or four years before I was guided to learn other things about connectedness. All my life's lessons were experiential, so it is no surprise that God was giving me a virtual buffet of gifts that I could eventually share with others. One thing was for sure, the moment Archangel Michael began bringing me very troubled, angry and evil souls for help and I began getting physically sick during the process, I asked that he stop. He stopped bringing souls right then.

Always curious, I kept notes on those many transitions including how each contacted me as well as additional information I was able to glean before sending them over. I thought it might be important one day, so I asked them what year they died, how they died, whether they were male or female, how many there were (group size), and then I noted why they were stuck. The information I received from them was amazing and enlightening. Who knows, I just might write another book about that someday.

To summarize, what I found was those who fail to transition and become stuck fall into one of more than fifteen categories from not being spiritual and believing there can be no life after death to having some sense of duty that binds them here to earth. Others are so codependent with someone who is also stuck or who remains on the earth-plane, that they can't let go and transition. That codependent category looks different from person to person. Sometimes it is between individuals and other times group loyalty; an example being when a team refuses to leave one another when they have all passed in some tragic accident. This could be a sports team, a military group or other powerful associations such as cults or religious orders where death comes to many at once. Sometimes it's simply intense fear that makes one soul stick like glue to another person still alive or to another soul who is also stuck.

Some spirits simply have hardened hearts and during the course of their lives have completely shut out love. It's therefore difficult for those souls to allow themselves to surrender to a place filled with unconditional love. There is also Florence's case, whereby she couldn't let go of material attachment. Others can simply be totally ignorant about the process, be completely analytical whereby if this hadn't made sense to them intellectually, they can't accept it when they die. Interestingly, it doesn't seem to matter if they are agnostic or atheist, as long as they can feel and receive love. Also not uncommon is feeling guilt and unworthiness to pass over. Finally, there are those souls who are being held back from transitioning by another soul, either through evil or some form of desperation. Or, like my son, the shock of his death simply left him stunned, confused and paralyzed by fear.

I was allowed these experiences and believe the lesson here is that the more we are aware of the magnificence of an afterlife and the love and healing that exists on the other side, the easier it will be for a quick and very easy journey. Like Marlene's mother in taking the express elevator. But, I believe most people take a day or two or three to transition. There is often shock and that delays the process for some, but not for long. Most people, with any amount of love in their hearts, are eventually drawn like magnets to the afterlife.

The last three decades of my life have been astounding to me and I'm amazed at the amount we all still have to learn about what is around us and what awaits us after. I'm so grateful I've had these experiences and know it's now my duty to share with others, but the experiences haven't stopped with transitioning spirits.

One thing I know for sure is ghost busters, or those who shoo away ghosts or spirits, are barbarians. These souls need help; they don't need to be chased away. The "Ghostbusters" movies were funny but absolutely nonsense. These souls are not troublemakers; they're merely signaling for help.

Other Messages Begin

After that, I moved on to another communication journey. At first it confused me. This one began in 2005, in fact November 28, 2005, since I wrote down my reaction and exactly what I heard at the time.

The smoke detector in my home when I lived on Exeter Boulevard in Scottsdale, was doing bizarre things; not the normal beeping from a dying battery. I didn't describe in the paper exactly what I had heard, but I did write down what I said aloud, in the event people had come to me for transitioning help.

"If there are spirits trying to reach me, please let me know now."

That was not the case this time. I can remember sitting at my small, round, glass breakfast table just off my kitchen. During this period in my life, I was caring for my favorite aunt, Aunt Minnie (Mildred Ouart), who lived in Illinois and was suffering from dementia. She was in her nineties and her dementia had been progressing over a ten-year period. I had been traveling back and forth to Illinois to make sure she was well and cared for. This message was about my Aunt Minnie. It was from her family, who had all died many years prior. They were asking me for help.

"Okay. We're here. We are family. Uncle Lee. Aunt Till. Grandma and Ray (Minnie's mother and former husband, also long since gone.). *We want to talk to you about Mill and your care for her. We love you a lot, Sandy, but we are worried about Mill and want you to help us help her."*

I asked if I had done something wrong and they continued,

"No, you are doing a great job but we see things you cannot see and we know things, watching her, you cannot know. The album was our idea. Put it together <u>soon</u> so you can send it to her before Christmas. Put us all in there. Dig out old pictures from everywhere. Have her miss us. We will help guide your hand. We want her with us and she is so, so, so lonely and simply miserable without her people. Help us Sandy."

A few days earlier an idea popped into my head for a Christmas gift for Aunt Minnie I thought she'd enjoy. A little four by six photo album (thirty-six pages) of old photos of her family that she could glance through and reminisce about. Her short-term memory was pretty much gone so she would often ask about her sister, her mother, her brother and others as if they were still here.

Once, Minnie told me she wanted to go visit Aunt Till, her sister, who had been dead for thirty years. Not to confuse or upset her, I'd say, "Great idea, we'll go after lunch." Meanwhile I knew she'd forget in twenty minutes but she'd stay happy in the short-term.

Telling her Till was gone would have been too traumatic for her. I made that mistake once and her reaction was like the first time she had heard the news; she cried and cried and was so upset. I couldn't cause her to grieve like that again. So, I stayed in her reality and that made us both happy.

That photo album would be perfect, I thought. Now I realize that idea wasn't mine at all. I guess I had a little help. Their message continued,

"Include old fishing photos, your folks, the people on Auburn Street, Pat and Andy, Bill and Betty, you know, the gang. Use

old-time photos so she'll keep looking at them and remembering us. Use very few current ones. Even include Lee's old wives (Lee was Mill's brother). *Please help us."*

I realized that Mill's time was drawing to an end and that having her connecting to joy and those she loved was a good thing. She could do that naturally by filling up with love while remembering those in her life who were no longer surrounding her physically. Her love would overtake the sadness, which would make her transitioning easier.

Now, do you see how it can be perfectly logical for souls on the other side to want to connect with us? Once in a while it is to give someone a message, like they are okay, they love them or they are grateful for something that person did. They also see what we do not. They are full of love and want to help but can only do so if we pay attention and are receptive. I was blessed to be able to do that.

Since 2005, I've heard from so many departed souls who've given me enormous insight about what lies beyond and how we can love and help one another, and from those who were just there to cheer me on and support me when I needed it. I went back and counted thirty-seven different souls who have popped in to connect over the years. There may be more.

Many came only once but some came multiple times. I'll be quoting a few of those as we proceed. Additionally, I've heard from four different angels, seven different entities (groups of very advanced souls), three other guides and five different Ascended Masters including Jesus and Buddha. God has also spoken through my heart and the Holy Spirit guides me daily.

The Greater Lesson

Now, remember this is not some gift that came to me through a near-death experience and not a gift I've had since birth. I wasn't able to begin connecting with the other side until I was in my forties. The process, however, really is not all that mysterious. It's normal and natural if we just relax and accept what we see and hear as "possible." Even decades before Jon died, weird things happened in my life and I was curious enough to ask if someone was trying to contact me. Someone most always was. But, in terms of those we love who have passed, most everybody I've ever talked to who has lost someone they cared about has a story. A story about how some strange coincidence happened which they believe might have been a signal from someone they loved who passed on. In my case, I was just willing to take everything to another level.

It's not critical to know right this minute the details of how all this connectedness works. It's more important to realize it just might be possible. If we can accept that, the rest of this book will make more sense. At that point I'll explain how I knew they were signaling me and how you can become more aware of this phenomenon too.

What is wise for you to hold on to now is that when loved ones reach out to you, the message doesn't have to be complex or prophetic. It can simply be to tell you how much they love you or thank you for something you did, or even more importantly, to tell you how sorry they are for something they did to you. One takeaway for all of us right here on earth is that guilt is not good. If possible it is better to rid our souls of guilt while on earth. The process is much easier when we can be face-to-face with someone and simply say we're sorry, cleanse our souls of the issue and move on. Or, forgive ourselves of whatever we feel guilty about. There are plenty of articles online or books you can pick up to help with that.

Eliminating guilt is very important for healing. Sometimes when guilt hasn't been relieved in this life, that same guilt accompanies a person to the other side. That's when it's more challenging to eliminate. Imagine the soul over there who wants so desperately to tell you how sorry they are but you just don't hear them or receive the messages they're trying to send. So, their cleansing process is more lengthy and complex than it needs to be.

Guilt also slows down the transitioning process for all of us to get to Heaven, as you remember. Some departing souls don't feel worthy enough for a speedy crossing. I've spent a bit of time on this to remind you that if you have a loved one who is now deceased, who might feel guilty about his or her role in your life, open your heart to the possibility that they might be wanting to say, "I'm so very sorry." Listen and watch for the signals. At least when a signal appears, say, "Thank you." Don't just ignore it.

Chapter 5
IT'S A MATTER OF ENERGY

I n the 1990's the study of quantum physics accelerated. This new science accepted that the universe, including us, is made up of energy, not matter. Quantum physics proved and continues to prove that solid matter does not exist in this universe. Atoms are not solid, in fact, they have three different subatomic particles inside them: protons, neutrons and electrons. The protons and neutrons are packed together into the center of the atom, while the electrons whiz around the outside. The electrons move so quickly that we never know exactly where they are from one moment to the next.[1] Many of us remember learning about protons, neutrons and electrons in high school science courses but not about quantum physics.

So, because there is only truly energy that exists, it obviously appears in a variety of forms. There's thermal (heat), chemical, nuclear, electrical, radiant, light, motion, elastic and gravitational, as well as sound energy. It makes sense to me that energy is the glue that binds us all together. But, there's one more form of energy that's not on that initial list. We can't forget the energy of love. That's the interesting one which we'll talk about later in this chapter.

Listen, I'm not a scientist or a scholar in quantum physics, but I am smart, and although I rarely play this card in this case I feel compelled to. I'm a member of MENSA and to get into that small, elite club one has to have an IQ in the upper two percent of the world's population. Since I have no PhD or masters degree in any subject being discussed in this book, I am writing from my personal experiences, from a deep knowing that comes from somewhere else. Most importantly, I am not some gullible dilettante playing around with metaphysics. I am, in fact, a critical thinker, analytical about practically everything and not a push-over for random theories. I'm proficient in problem solving and linking complex ideas together in a logical form, as well as in simplifying the very complicated. Those are my intellectual gifts.

This digression is to make the point that in the event someone reading this book believes I'm just repeating something I've read or parroting something I've heard from some weird New Age group, that's absurd. I'm pretty much a skeptic. The exception to rarely believing what I hear is when it comes from a highly credible source, and even then that subject has to make sense to me, generally thorough my own investigation. Whatever the information is, the dots have to connect in my mind. When it comes to connecting the dots among energy, frequency, human vibration and the existence of other dimensions, all those dots connect for me.

If nothing else, my own experience, even though it was accidental, reinforces much of this in my mind. Then, science and theories like those from quantum physics are added to the mix. Layer that with the messages that have actually been communicated to me from those who have passed, and the foundation for all my conclusions becomes more solid. But I think the initial prompting for me to put all this in writing was the culmination of messages over the years from souls explaining and reinforcing "the way it is." The final catalyst was my son's passing and the clarity with which Jon communicates to me about anything I ask, and the fact that he begged me to explain to people about connecting dimensions and express that this process is possible.

Jon's clarity in everything he shares comes from the fact that our relationship back and forth is just that, a relationship. We talk, I ask questions and he answers, and so on. Others from the other side who also appear in my life offer advice, and sometimes I ask a few questions, but never home in on a subject the way I do with Jon. With my son I have a baseline, as it were, on which to build future questions and clarify issues that are so very complex, it takes quite a bit of drilling down until these concepts can be simply understood by us mortals. Most importantly, Jon wants to help.

Energy is the Easiest Signal to Use

Since energy is the great connector it makes perfect sense that energy would be the method by which dimensions can most easily interact. So, when souls want to attract our attention, they typically use some form of energy to make that happen. Jon's energy link takes the form of messing around with frequencies that typically cause quite a disruption in my life to ensure I don't miss recognizing he's there. But many busy people still don't "get it."

Let me give you a few examples of how their playing with energy creates signals for us: computers acting so whacky like a key will automatically repeat, a word document will refuse to close, or spacing will jump all over the place. With cell phones it could be repeating texts, but always the unexpected and unexplained. TVs act up and electrical systems in cars go awry too. Smoke detectors act bizarrely, light bulbs might flash or suddenly go on or off and in one particular case, and almost always when I take a walk, streetlights that go on and off are one of Jon's favorites. Since we're surrounded by electrical energy here on earth, electrical connections are often the easiest way for them to attract the most attention.

When I asked Jon if he connected with others besides me, this is how he replied:

> *"Well, I just shout and throw things but nobody pays much attention."*

I felt his smile. What he was actually saying is that people are either closed off to the possibility, too busy, don't recognize a signal when they see it or are too distracted with everyday life to pay attention. That, I'm afraid, is probably the norm.

I'll give you another example. I'm one of those busy people. I don't notice little flashing subtleties that pop into my life, but I do notice something that interferes with my routine. One day I was sitting at my computer, and you know how we all have lots of file folders and documents on our desktops? Well, I have way too many—probably between sixty-five and seventy. I'm always working on many projects at once and have lots of files out for reference. Well, when I sat down, it was like an eruption of files. Every one of them opened up at the exact same time; exploding on the screen in an uncontrollable fashion with documents fanning across the desktop, one on top of the other like one would fan a deck of cards. I was frantic and couldn't close them quickly enough. For every one that I closed, ten more would open. Finally I yelled,

"Stop."

But nothing worked. Then I asked,

"Honey, is that you?"

"*Yes Momma, it's me,*" was the answer.

"Please stop this, I'll be right there. Please stop,"

I said very loudly so he'd hear me; and he finally did. As always, I grabbed my pen and tablet and sat down to take notes on what my son had to say next.

Now, somebody else would think that was a computer issue, a short or something, and shut the computer down, swear at the screen or call the Geek Squad. Even if they did call for help, there most always wouldn't be a good explanation for what had occurred. The least likely explanation can often be the most likely. So, weird behavior from a computer is a very typical signal. There are endless other examples. Sometimes it is not a spirit calling out, sometimes it's just a physical problem. But most of the time it's my friends, family and others from the other dimensions. If you want to know for sure, ask.

There Are Other Ways to Connect Too

Souls try and do make a connection with us in other ways too. Perhaps a person sees a vision, or has a physical-type encounter in which they might have feelings that someone is in the room with them or even smell a fragrance their loved one always wore. Perhaps a person just feels a sudden chill or warmth that comes over them—not hot flashes, ladies—or something out of the normal, like with a sudden breeze.

My friend Susan saw lilacs blooming near her mother's grave when they were totally out of season. Lilacs were Susan's favorite flower. Another friend, this one a male, is often visited by hummingbirds, his mother's favorite bird. "Visited" may not be the right description. When hiking in the desert, where you'd never expect to see a hummingbird, one would appear, and once the little beauty just stayed fluttering right in front of Wayne's face for what seemed like many minutes. He talked to it and it just stayed right in front of his nose, looking him right in the eyes. Odd? Not really when you consider that maybe Wayne's mom wanted to say hello or just check in. Wayne's a smart guy though and figured that out all by himself.

Of course there are also dream visits, which are not uncommon at all. Many people I know have told me about seeing a loved one in their dream, sometimes just smiling and other times bringing a loving message. Never menacing dreams—always kind and loving appearances.

When I asked Jon if he and other souls become frustrated or are sad when they're unable to connect with someone here, he said that isn't the case:

> "Not like you do. It's just a bounce back (for us). You try and it works or it doesn't. If you are determined, you keep trying different ways or with more energy. Some up here have more determination than others. Some are tired, some are weak (or gentle), and

some move past these connections 'cause they were irrelevant in the life they just had. Like you wouldn't connect with a neighbor just because you knew them. If they weren't part of your story or in the same vibrational pattern, they become irrelevant later."

The Radar Screen

I know energy is key to all of this because in messages I've heard from several friends who have contacted me after moving on, there has been a general reference to it. One such friend, Marcia, said she saw me on the radar screen. Several people have used that terminology, so here are a couple brief examples.

I was contacted once by a very prominent national figure with whom I instantly connected the first time we met. I'll keep from referencing his name because it really doesn't change the story one way or the other. Anyway, this man ended up being an admirer of sorts and we kept running into each other when he'd speak at national political events held here in Phoenix. No question there was some type of chemistry or something going on, in fact, the first time he saw me his reaction was anything but subtle.

Prior to a major speech here, this attractive and charismatic man entered the ballroom where four hundred to five hundred people were all seated at ten-top tables for the evening event. He was very handsome and meandered amongst the tables greeting the seated guests as he made his way to the podium. About three rows of tables into the process, when our eyes connected, something instantly happened to him. He lost focus and made a beeline directly to my table. It was amazing and funny to watch. He passed several tables in between us and headed straight for where my husband and I were seated. I don't think he even saw or cared that my husband was sitting next to me. He just kept walking directly to where I was. As he greeted folks at our table, he never took his eyes off me. Even when he spoke from the podium, he kept turning, much more frequently than a normal rotation of the body, toward where I was. It really was funny, flattering and obvious.

Now, a person might say, "Sandy, you're thinking pretty highly of yourself." But that wasn't even on my mind, it was just impossible to ignore. My husband brought it up later and laughed because he was absolutely stunned too.

The few other times we attended an event where this national politician was the speaker, Steve would always comment, "There's your boyfriend." And, the same sort of things would happen. If the truth was told, I did have a bit of a crush on this fellow. He was a charmer. He was very good-looking, and well respected on both sides of the aisle. Of course he was a politician but had also been a very dashing football quarterback in his day. I was shocked when after he died, he contacted me. When I asked how he had found me, this is what he said:

> *"The radar screen. Up here, there is a way to zip through lots of your life and pick up energies that are responsive to connection and <u>there you were!</u> Not many in the political arena or even pro sports are open to what you can do or are able to receive. WOW, was I pleasantly surprised. It was like seeing you for the first time at that speaking event in Phoenix. I'm so happy I know you are there."*

There was much more to the message and although he and I never got to spend any time together in this lifetime, we did chat a bit across dimensions. It was all very flattering and sweet ☺ .

Another friend, a woman about ten years older than I am who passed when she was in her early seventies, came to me a number of years ago. Her name was Marcia and she was gorgeous her entire life, simply gorgeous. She came to explain why she had left and for me to give messages to two of her girlfriends. I couldn't find the one friend and the other never returned any of my messages, so I'm afraid I disappointed Marcia. But, in the course of that contact she managed to make clever, cute comments like she was known to do. She had a wonderful sense of humor besides being a stunning beauty.

"No, I really had no serious message. Someone had you on the radar screen so I thought I'd chime in."

That was how she explained the connection. She continued to tell me that she *"liked my shoes,"* which was a running joke between us since we would often show up at some social event wearing with the exact same shoes. We both had great taste. Ha!

So, I asked Jon if there was a radar screen up there and he shared:

"Oh, like when Marcia said you showed up on the radar screen? That is like a reverse of what I just said. This time we tune in to our life team, or to people we have ever touched in any way. They are all available and some shine brighter, so we know we can connect. That is what you do. Shine brightly up here . So those you knew or met can connect if they need to or want to. Generally, it's the former, unless they were love connections,"

Another time when Jon and I were talking, we were talking about how souls connect with us and Jon referenced the radar screen metaphor again:

"We do see energetic paths – kind of like a radar screen, but no physical screen. Some paths are very familiar, like with you. Sometimes there are no paths to people we love 'cause they don't exist directly and we have to use unique routes to make a connection happen; like friends who know friends. Some paths have blockages and it's frustrating to see those—like where people are too busy; minds are too active; not paying attention or totally unaware. You want to take a drill and drill those, but it can't be done from up here."

Jon was referencing how sometimes someone a soul may want to reach is inaccessible because they are unwilling or unable, so they go through another person who is open, who knows the inaccessible one. Then the soul asks that a message be delivered to the mutual acquaintance.

That would explain the way the Long Island Medium and many mediums who use public forums are able to do the work they do. If a soul is longing to connect with someone on earth and that person is either in the audience or in the presence of the Long Island Medium, for example selling her shoes or whatever, the medium is often compelled to share the message because the soul connects with the medium.

Jon continued with a request that I simply could not refuse.

> "That is why I want you to do work to help people open up, so we can all connect. We all need to be together to benefit each other and so that love can flow freely between dimensions. We are supposed to be connected."

This was one of many times Jon has asked me to please speak on or write about this subject. Now, I ask, how can I say no to a request like that?

One other time I was contacted by a woman who departed in 2013, and who I had known through social circles. Her name was Carole. She came to me to talk about some common experiences we had together; for instance, sitting near each other when we both had floor seats for the Phoenix Mercury women's basketball games. She asked that I pass on a message to a social couple that were friends of hers. In the course of her message to me she said something that again reinforced the energy connection:

> "Contact kind of pops up in our energy field. Can't explain it but everybody we've ever connected with is energetically there and those who can be connected with or are connecting with others up here are kind of highlighted. Not in print but in awareness. Again, can't explain it but I know sooooo many who would love to know this is possible."

Some souls on the other side are very evolved, and some are more in the beginning stages. Some grasp all of the intricacies in an instant about all this, and others struggle to understand those complexities themselves while trying to explain it to us.

This woman did not bring the clarity Jon eventually did about the same issue, but her energy reference was very, very similar to many I've heard. Later it in her message, Carole let me know that sharing messages from a couple of others was also perfectly fine.

"Well Sandy, signing off now. And Glenna and Marcia have no problem if you share. Don't know about Susan. If you can help others and bring them peace, go for it! Love to my "almost" friend, Carole."

That message came in April, 2013.

Brighter Lights

Jon also said more to me about how our departed recognize with whom they can connect. It is all very complex which is why Jon brought the subject up over and over to me. Here is a sample of his progression of explanations on the subject:

"The individuals in our 'life team' are all energetically connected, even over here." *"We tune in to our 'life team' or people we have ever touched in any way. They are all available and some shine brighter, so we can connect."*

Another time he explained even more clearly:

"It's like flying into a city and seeing all the lights beneath. Everyone we have ever known in our lives is represented. Those we have simply met only once, dealt with casually or observed from afar, but who still impacted our lives. They are all there—our loved

ones, our family—everyone in our earth-experience tribe whose interaction was a part of this existence. They all show up as little lights but some of those lights shine brighter. Those are the ones we can connect with."

This is particularly relevant to me since so many who work in related spiritual fields, healing arts or other caring professions are often referred to as "light workers." Fascinating description, isn't it?

Love Energy

When we try to understand the many forms of energy, love cannot be ignored. Love is considered by some to be the most divine energy of all. So those with open hearts and in the love space vibrate at a higher level, or frequency, than others. I don't mean "in love" in terms of being in a love relationship with another human being, but rather living in a state of unconditional love. No one can deny that God is love in its purest form: bliss, divine and unconditionally loving. That is the frequency many spiritual seekers here on earth try to attain, or to become as close as possible to on this plane. Raising one's frequency isn't a foreign concept because the higher the frequency, the more pure the soul is.

If your goal is to raise your frequency higher, there are a number of behaviors that are beneficial: appreciate beauty; drink plenty of water; meditate; be grateful; practice acts of kindness; and think, say and feel generous loving thoughts—all of these help. However, love is the most powerful method for raising the human frequency. We do that with an open heart so we can receive even more than we can generate.

When we think of the greatest teachers who ever walked the earth, many seemed to have glowed. Those individuals were all filled with love, unconditional love—love that everyone around them felt and of which people near them could simply not get enough. So, when a soul attains that state, the state of complete unconditional love, I'm told rewards in Heaven are possible.

As near perfection as Jesus was, for example, as well as other Ascended Masters, none was as pure a hundred percent of the time as God. All had taken a human form with all the temptations, imperfections and challenges that life presents. Some had flashes of doubt, frustration, fear and all the other emotions that cause us to react in ways that are not completely perfect. All those negative feelings are the antithesis of love. And for God, love is all there is. It would be wise for that to be the human goal as well.

God created us in His image but we have to grow into that, I'm afraid. The spark may have been pure when we were created, but we certainly screw it up along the way. Given free will, we simply mess things up by living our lives. So, to grow into perfection—loving all unconditionally, being helpful and kind to everyone we meet, without judging—is a continual growth process. We notice those imperfections within ourselves when we transition and somehow our souls always strive for the perfection that a higher frequency (of love) will bring—the perfect state. Jon explained this in an interesting way, especially when I asked him if he got to see God:

> "It's not like that. He allows total freedom and self-will at the soul level too. I guess there may be one more level when a soul is more like a master teacher. Then they rest together, with Him, and then they (the souls) are through. There are many more than the ones (Master Teachers) people refer to, more common-type ones (souls). They are all there too and will never come back."

Jon was talking about Ascended Masters and Master Teachers including just very pure souls who lived on earth and were never formally recognized but were always guided by love. He may have been talking about traditional angels and saints as well. Jon continued:

> "But most of us spirit schleps appear to be on the next floor down—or several down; an elevator analysis—get it?"

Jon's directness was generally laced with a light heart and a smile. I'm so happy he never lost that quality. Summarizing the soul growth situation on the other side, I loved this analysis of his the best:

"I'll tell you, God is universal everywhere (up here) *and at all frequencies, degrees and levels. He touches the weak, fearful, satanic and angels. Doesn't matter. It's a matter of* (personal) *access. Kind of like you are swimming underwater in a clear, magnificent stream and you're thirsty, but you're swimming with your mouth shut. Some idiots die from dehydration 'cause they never open their mouths to take a drink while in this unbelievable environment. Others develop gills and absorb the moisture that way, with mouths open once in a while and eventually* (they absorb) *through their skin. They actually become the love* (God) *that surrounds them."*

Jon went on to say,

"So, I feel God every second to my capacity at this point in my soul's growth and eventually I'll become a fish up here. Ha! Ha!"

What a wonderful illustration, I thought. Jon continued,

"Make sense? Everything is so clear up here and these kinds of parables are the same Masters have used for centuries to illustrate points. You can use mine, whenever. Well, not really mine, but...."

When Jon references Masters and Master Level Teachers he is talking about those who are still living on this earth. They are few and far between. That title is not automatically given to someone who happens to be in the clergy, and not even to those who concentrate on rituals or readings or follow strict guidelines they understand intellectually. That title is reserved for people who live in love. They receive and accept divine guidance constantly. They never question it nor try to understand life experiences or why they happen. They have total faith and trust in God and every day are like an open channel from which God's love flows, or overflows, on to everyone they meet. Pope John Paul II immediately comes to mind. The (14th) Dalai Lama is another, pure love, both of them.

I have probably known two or three such people in my entire life; simple, regular people where the state of love was just normal for them and they brought joy to everyone they touched.

What About Religion Over There?

I finally got around to asking if there was religious separation over there. His answer was fascinating since some religions teach that only through their way can one reach God and Heaven. I was curious about Jon's experience. His answer was very direct:

"There is no religion here. No groupings by religious sects. Jesus, Buddha and other true Masters are ascended to a higher plane (love energy, frequency) than most of us. There are layers like in this hologram. We can cross through to touch or see, but we exist where we have earned. That's why people come back to ascend at a higher frequency, so they can hang with the big dogs."

I laughed out loud. Finally, Jon concluded,

"God's energy, however, permeates everything. Hard for mortals to grasp but its kind of degrees of bliss. People only end up to the max of what they can comprehend or feel in the earth experience, or I should say life experience. I'll share more about that later.

I think my son was hinting at life in other portions of the Universe or Universes.

Chapter 6
LIFE'S "TIME-OUTS" BRING SPIRITUAL GIFTS

S ome people may never wake up and find themselves able to connect to the other side or have premonitions about what may or may not happen in the future, like mediums and psychics claim. In fact, I don't believe most people wake up to those gifts at all. I believe we all have that ability but because of fear, religious teachings or being unwilling to open ourselves to love, unconditionally, those gifts never develop. I also believe that the ability for connecting with other dimensions grows once an individual embraces the love of God and a closeness to Him that makes them totally surrender to whatever the Good Lord may have in store for them to experience.

Surrender is a challenge for most people because it makes them vulnerable. But, vulnerability comes naturally when a person is faced with long "time-outs" in their lives or a sudden shock or trauma that makes them reach out to a Higher Source in a profound way.

I believe connectedness to the other side or other talents that begin to use the enormous gifts God gave us often develop as a result of circumstances, or an incident that wakes us up spiritually. For some, such an event could be a sudden shock. For others, a critical illness or devastating disability that forces them to reach out to God in desperation. For still others it could be in deep sorrow or loneliness that causes them to call out to God for answers and for love. Or, for some it might just be lingering solitude that draws them nearer to their Lord and Savior. Some reach out to God directly and some through Jesus Christ or another religious entity in which they believe.

Lingering solitude often creates an environment in which a person begins to feel more connected to God or to develop a spiritual awakening. By lingering solitude I'm referring to a form of isolation that pulls us from our day-to-day world, not just living alone as a single person. I'm referring to a person who is convicted of a crime, justly or unjustly, and is locked away in a prison where life is a set routine, is very simply lived and which offers plenty of alone time. That's one example.

That's why some incarcerated individuals find religion, become born again or become students of the Bible, because they have much time for self-reflection. These people often come closer to God, and through daily communication they unburden their souls and free themselves to receive not only God's blessings but often more.

Solitude can also be the result of a chronic or critical illness or accident that requires lengthy hospital stays, long periods away from normal life and a new existence that removes them from their daily rituals for weeks, months or years. When such events occur, it's not unusual for such people to cry out for help and turn to God. Again, with adequate time for self-reflection, repentance and a new yearning for closeness to the Lord, some find that closeness and they might also find something else.

Tragedy too brings many much nearer to their Creator. When grief and deep sorrow overtake a person and that person cries out for help, it isn't always the horizontal connections in life that are the most comforting, sometimes it is the vertical ones. When answers from a vertical source of any kind occur through flashes of insight or comforting words from somewhere unidentified, some people sadly ignore or dismiss them. But the lucky few who accept those comforting words feel much better and more at peace as a result. We don't always have to understand the how and the why of things that occur in our life, but trust and faith make life much easier.

Let me share a personal story about the first time I ever heard a "voice" speaking to me. Even though it came through my own head, it was not from my conscious mind. I was five years old and had just woken up in the morning after an experience the night before that was so traumatic to me that it was a "blackout" event in my consciousness. My mom recounted the "blackout" experience to me when I was grown and it sounded very familiar as she shared it. But I have no clear recollection of that event at all, except for the message I received the next morning. That message came loud and clear, and when I think back, I still hear it today.

Every evening my mother would sit on the edge of my bed and tell me stories about when she was a little girl, stories about my father's younger years and both sets of stories were always fascinating—not always wonderful—but always true. My mother also had a thing about lying and one of her strongest values was honesty and truthfulness.

Sometimes, along with those stores, I'd ask questions and she'd reply.

This particular evening, I asked, as many little kids might do, if I was adopted. I don't know why that thought even popped into my head, but it did. Don't think I noticed that my mom was short, had dark eyes and hair, and my Dad was about five-eleven with dark eyes and dark hair too, while I was blonde and blue-eyed and appeared as though I'd become quite a tall girl when I grew up. None of that entered my mind and I never realized the distinction. I was just curious and blurted out the question.

My mother had never told me anything about the possibility of being adopted and not being her biological child. Nor did she ever volunteer the information until I was eighteen. My parents were sweet, simple people who were ignorant about how to manage such a subject with their daughter, and thought they had years to confront the issue. Both had eighth-grade educations and were ill-equipped for a shocking question like that being thrown at them from out of the blue, with me being so young. Later I came to recognize that the reason my adoption was never discussed was that my mother feared I would no longer love her and would search for and love my biological mother instead. So, my precious mother never addressed the subject. Then that very question popped out of my mouth and my mom, who would have rather chewed broken glass than tell a lie, was forced to answer:

"Yes,"

That was all she said. My eyes widened and I started jabbering about my dog Lucky, the next day at school, what we were going to have for dinner and any number of rambling topics that erased from my mind what I had just heard. And my sweet and very fearful mother said nothing more. She just let me ramble on and on until I became tired and finally fell asleep.

I don't remember any of that experience, but I do remember the next morning waking up, stepping on to the throw rug in my bedroom and hearing a voice say to me,

"You are special."

I was never someone with a big ego and I never thought I was better than anyone else— no matter what I ever achieved in the way of recognition or acclaim. So, as I grew up and remembered the message I had heard that morning, I never took it personally. Instead, I thought it meant I would do something special with my life or I was to accomplish something big during my life. That voice was always with me, and maybe because of that, throughout my life I latched on to big challenges fearlessly.

Many years later when I was seventy, God came to me in a message to remind me to see the possibilities and potential in my life when I was very stressed about my finances. This is how He closed the three-page communication:

"Just stopped by to remind you that you are special, my dear Sandy. It is my voice you heard those many years ago and you have made me proud. Your Father."

I digress with this personal story to make the point that for too many people, the thought that God could actually directly give them comfort or advice totally eludes them. That all those years ago I knew my message was from someone and it was important. That was all I needed at that age. Today, when I hear a direct, short and relevant message, I smile. I now assume it is the Holy Spirit guiding me, comforting me and giving me an "attagirl" once in a while. Once you realize a connection has actually been made, it isn't difficult to maintain that connection and allow it to enrich your life.

So, trauma or shock or these lengthy breaks in the rituals of daily life might really be meant to connect us to what we would be wisest to connect to. Anyway, that's something to think about. So, if something plucks you from the treadmill of life and gives you pause, be grateful for the experience. Instead of cursing the pitfalls of the incident or experience and being impatient for your routine to begin again, recognize that this might be a very important time for you to learn and grow.

Here's a great example, the COVID-19 pandemic and subsequent stay-at-home orders we received state by state in the Spring of 2020 devastated so many people. Folks were totally bored without having the company of friends and family. Yet, some of us were thrilled. The slower pace, the quiet and solitude was a gift to refresh and recharge. Everyone was given a chance to reflect, to reconnect with themselves, to reach out for spiritual guidance and to enrich their souls. Unfortunately, I think I and a handful of others were in the minority.

Over the years I've heard God's voice many times; generally in short messages, but most always in response to a pleading for comfort. I've also noticed that God truly does have a wonderful sense of humor. I first noticed that prior to writing my first book when I was searching for various answers and He gave me a few. I was, of course, grateful and remember once asking (back in 2007) if I could ever quote Him:

> "Sure. Not convinced everyone will believe you, but use my name if you wish (humor)."

The humor was part of His message that day and I thought it was funny He wanted to clarify that with the parenthetical.

About the same time, while I was still working on my first book and doing what I believed was His work, at least work He had inspired me to do, I was stressing over money from a client that I had not yet received.

"Don't you realize my child, when you work for me you always get paid? That's a little Heavenly Humor."

I think He got a kick out of being funny and always wanted to make sure I laughed.

My Gifts Came From Illness

It's indisputable that my thirty-five years of living with illness and pain, in many forms, brought me to where I am today. And, because I always seemed to recognize the miracle of the body and trusted God to lead me to what I needed and when I needed it, He took me on this marvelous journey.

Through facing pain without drugs, I learned to clear my mind. I later recognized that such pain mitigation was possible within the process of meditation. Through that discipline, I also found a new way to communicate and to receive. No experience is by accident. And through that blessing, ever since I learned to connect, I've been able to face the loss of the most precious gift I was ever given in this life, my son Jon.

Although Jon's passing was devastating, the moment I heard him call out to me I knew I was still connected to him. I didn't consciously think about that connection but I "felt" connected. That connectedness has never stopped. I eventually realized Jon was not gone from me; he had merely shifted to another form. I never could have found that connectedness without everything I experienced through all of the lengthy and lingering illness I have faced in life.

Recovering from Addiction Might Bring Blessings as Well

Before I forget, I must include one other form of "time-out"; the "time-out" that those facing addiction face when trying to fully recover. First detox and then rehab, both of which are needed to cleanse the body and realign one's focus. I believe one of the most successful methods for treating those addicted to alcohol is Alcoholics Anonymous (AA), those addicted to drugs Narcotics Anonymous (NA), and spin-off programs for those addicted to gambling, Gamblers Anonymous (GA), etc. All these "Anonymous" programs are based on a twelve-step process that stresses how helpless we all are without help from a Higher Power. The founders of AA knew there was a thirst for a spiritual connection with those facing any form of addiction, and that the community these programs provide, which individuals can access almost anytime, are filled with forgiveness, letting go of judgment and an outpouring of love within a tight knit community of like souls.

The eighth step is particularly important to those who participate, and important for all of us, even those not in the program. That step deals with making amends to individuals we have wronged because of the addiction. We all might consider how making amends helps alleviate guilt, and might remember what I mentioned earlier about how important eliminating guilt is at the soul level.

The connection with God, or your Higher Power, helps facilitate peace and contentment in life. Once the connection with God has been made, it's impossible not to realize how much we are loved by Him every day and for all eternity. The spiritual connection and feeling and receiving of love are links to Heaven we can all experience right here on earth.

Time-outs, isolation, desperation and tragedy are all motivators to reach out to God and to encourage us to make the connection we are all meant to have. The Divine connection allows us to feel constant love and support from our Creator, and opens the channels to feel love to the degree our souls are capable.

It's not really difficult to see how a gift like I have now can creep up on someone in the course of a challenging life. Once a person realizes how connected they are to their Creator, the surrender begins. Then, when people are open to receiving, they do.

Chapter 7
THE POWER OF CONNECTEDNESS

onnectedness erases any feelings of loneliness that might exist in a person's life. Perhaps that's why I'm never lonely. I just open my heart and receive love from everywhere that's constantly flowing to me. It's then I feel most warm and content, and can't wait to share that love with others.

Sometimes I feel like I have a cast of hundreds around me all the time offering guidance, love and support. Now I have Jon too. However, the connection I have with my son is more like a relationship between dimensions than just a connection as I mentioned before. So, instead of jumping in and out of my life over the months or years, like others do, it's different with Jon. Sometimes I am pitiful, and when I am so very sad and crying, he will come to help. Other times he just checks in to see how I am and to offer his two cents on something that's going on. He often comments on his children, or on someone with whom I have a relationship, or on some special event I've attended. Sometimes it's simply someone he's happy to see around me.

The New Soul Connection

As I said before, Jon's relationship with me today is more consistent and complete than it was before his adult life got in the way. So, for those of you who have loved a child or spouse or family member or simply had a love connection that was incredibly strong and that person has left this earth, have no fear; that love never ends. One of the most powerful messages God has ever given me was this one:

"Loss is impossible in my world."

He is right. The body may leave but the love never does. It's the glue that connects us forever, soul to soul for all of eternity. The souls of our loved ones are always nearby watching us, cheering us on, celebrating our victories, reaching in to comfort us and loving us unconditionally and eternally. Even if in this life the relationship was bumpy or cruel or a major disappointment to you, once the soul reaches the other side that person changes. At that point, they're now able to connect with you in a way that's totally pure.

I say that because I know of a friend who told me how wretched her mother was to her throughout their life together. Another friend conveyed how abusive her husband had been. For some reason, both these women believed that their family members were still the same way, even though they're long-departed. Their belief is not accurate.

The most redeeming and beautiful thing about passing on to the next realm is that with transition, when one's life garments fall away and the soul becomes totally exposed, the person we love returns to purity. Heaven is much different than it is here. Souls are more reflective, more thoughtful, more kind and loving. They remain that way for all time and forever—until they return to a lifetime on earth—and then they forget who they really are and begin the lesson they set out to learn.

Our loved ones may have seemed ignorant on earth but trust me they become more wise on the other side. Though they seemed cruel on this plane, they become gentle in the other dimension. They are now authentic to their soul, which is a lot more beautiful than human life.

My relationship with Jon is now more active and sincere than the one I had with when he was fourteen to forty-six. Prior to Jon passing two years later, we drew quite a bit closer since he lived with me. During those previous years, however, he was busy with his life and had little time for me, which I guess isn't uncommon with sons and daughters through their twenties, thirties and forties. He also pushed himself away as much as he could.

Jon pretty much summed up our relationship on June 15, 2019 when he said to me:

> *"Now it* (our relationship) *is best. We have the purest, best love in the world—soul connected. You see the perfection in me and I see the perfection in you. Gosh, it's great. And, our lives don't get in the way, our attitudes don't get in the way, our moods don't get in the way and our mouths and actions don't hurt one another. You were right when you described this process to others. That is just the way this is—perfection from birth to about six and then, not so much.☺ Now, perfection again."*

He signed off with,

> *"Your favorite son, Jon."*

Now my son is focused on his soul growth, watching over those he loves, making amends and spreading love and joy where he can. So he comes to me when he wants to share something or when I need him most. He always just seems to know.

Being Lonely

Besides my routine contact with Jon and also others, most every morning I wake up speaking to both God and Jesus each day. I often see the face of Jesus in my mind and if I don't, I ask for that to happen, which always brings a big smile to my face. Then, I read a page from *Jesus Calling*, a wonderful little book of daily messages, and talk to God and the Holy Spirit asking for guidance so my day serves Him. I start the day connected and feeling very much loved. With all of these things going on in my life, it's impossible to be lonely.

That just happens to be my routine and just because Jesus might be one of my "go-to" voices on the other side, I have not totally ignored Buddha, Mother Mary, Isis or even a representative of the Hindu faith—all of whom have come to give me guidance, direction and messages to present within this book. So hopefully you'll find voices that resonate with you here as well. As long as we make positive vertical connections, it's impossible to feel alone.

How Society has Encouraged Separation

Yet, today society has developed into something that encourages separation, chases God from everyday life and fosters loneliness. The community that many people have found in their churches and other community "places" are disappearing. We fence our yards so we barely know our neighbors, we spend countless hours online with a remote view of the world and maintain a very superficial connection to those we like or love. Our phone calls are less frequent, texting more prevalent and personal meetings more rare. At family gatherings kids, adolescents and teens seem to have their faces buried in their cell phones. Actually, so do some of their parents.

All of this impersonality makes me feel sorry for young people today. When a person reduces communication to brief texts and 280 characters in a tweet, their communication skills suffer. I think everyone would agree that the grammar and spelling of people now under forty is dreadful (our education system is another subject)! Our kids have become distanced from others by the technology that is supposed to connect us. That disconnectedness makes it very, very difficult to spread love to others—sincere heart-open love can only be "felt" when someone is standing near. You can always text a heart to someone but who knows if it is really sincere or merely convenient. When they are in your presence and you feel that love, that's when you truly know.

No wonder so many people have become depressed and feel alone. Over the last two decades that has fostered the increase of suicide rates substantially.[2] In fact, the number of people taking their own lives is the highest it's been since World War II.[3] I believe technology-driven isolation and a lack of physical connectedness, as well as the trend toward a more secular society, have also contributed to our increase in accidental drug-related deaths. Drugs become a quick fix to mitigate the pain too many feel who are lonely, and hungry for feeling loved.

Isolation, Love and Addiction

The opioid crisis this world is facing is a fairly recent phenomenon, but one I believe is exacerbated by people feeling unloved and not needed. Sure, we can blame physicians for overprescribing, horrible childhoods and other reasons why a person might succumb to addiction, but I believe the causes are always more complex and much deeper. It isn't a coincidence than when an addict finds spiritual connection through a program like Alcoholics Anonymous (AA), recovery is much more likely to occur. That program happens to have a spiritual base and allows those who surrender to the existence of a power greater than themselves to feel wrapped in the love and security that many of the participants desperately need. Finding God, or whatever they describe as their Higher Power, as well as the fellowship of community gatherings (meetings) that are routine in such a program also foster a love connection among like souls.[4]

In terms of helping a loved one with addiction, as much as parents or loved ones try to help, it's impossible. Nobody can make that decision for another person especially if addiction is a path that some souls need to experience in order to learn something, to grow somehow or to live this journey in order to complete their life story. The painful part is that some of us can only watch.

I know with my precious son, feeling truly loved was missing in his life. Not that people didn't adore Jon, it was that I'm not sure Jon really felt it. Jon also had no strong spiritual connectedness. I think he tried going to church periodically, but it never truly resonated with him. After his passing, he told me how shocked he was to see the throngs of people at his funeral. He had no idea that many people truly cared about him.

Jon's issues were not based on any attachment to the world of technology, although he did love his cell phone; it began for him many years before texting, Facebook and the like. Technical isolation isn't always the cause. Sometimes not having a spiritual link to some power greater than oneself, and not feeling the love, is the root of the issue. Even folks immersed in organized religions can fail to receive God's love. People who need love the most can be surrounded by it, but like Jon stated earlier, they can be swimming in God's love with their mouths closed and become dehydrated. So sad, when all they have to do is open their mouths and drink.

Sometimes connecting vertically is less threatening and easier for these individuals than connecting horizontally. With human relationships, we experience the disappointments that occur frequently. So, even for those of us who are not addicted but lack the love we truly crave, the love of God and the love of those who have passed can fill the hole that might exist in day-to-day living. It's simply just a matter of connecting.

Jon shared something about his addiction experience that might be appropriate at this point. On December 21, 2018 he came to me and this was part of his message:

> "You don't know how lonely it is with addiction. We wall everyone out. We focus on the 'feel good'. We hurt so much and don't know how to feel better. We don't know how to even talk about how we really feel. At least, that was me."

Prayer and Connectedness

Another example of how being connected heals spiritually is the magic of prayer, especially intercessory prayer, for those with all types of health conditions including mental and emotional health. When others come together lovingly to solicit mercy and healing on someone else's behalf, the power of that solicitation is undeniable. We may not be aware of the prayers that are being said on our behalf, but our souls feel it. Intercessory prayer often works miracles. Prayer for another connects us in magical ways and spreads love worldwide.

I made prayer and connectedness a separate subset so I could share just a little about how prayer can open us up, regardless of who or what we pray to. God or the Universe seems to be the most common reference to having some hand in our lives, I just prefer God. With love and a sincere heart, we can ask to be led by the Holy Spirit with the help of angels and saints to make each day much easier and effortless.

I have three archangels who seem to like me and have been in my life for many years: Archangel Michael, Archangel Gabriel and Archangel Raphael. Of course I just call them Michael, Gabriel and Raphael. I thank them repeatedly for the little things they do for me to make life easier. If I explained about good parking spaces, you'd truly think I was nuts so I won't go there, but over the years I've just come to expect that I'll find the perfect parking spot and I always do. With a grateful heart, I thank Michael, Gabriel and Raphael each time.

Now, although you might believe in angels, you could also be one of those people who thinks a person shouldn't make common or ordinary requests like helping with a parking spot or other trivial matters, but angels really don't care. They don't judge what's important and what's not. They're just happy to help and cannot step in unless they're asked for assistance. So, any request can be honored—If you are grateful in advance and ask—knowing that whatever little thing you need will come.

Of course, none of this works unless you can accept that there may truly be something existing on the other side, and through that connection your prayer or request might be answered.

Filling the Hole in Your Heart

Prior to Jon's death, if anyone would have asked me how to help a grieving parent, husband or wife, lover or friend, I wouldn't have known how to answer. Today, it's a different matter. If the person remaining on earth feels like there is unfinished business with a loved one or friend who passed, there is something that can be done to remedy that.

I have a particular friend who asked me to lunch one day and told me about a girlfriend of hers who had passed away. My friend shared that she felt like the relationship was unfinished somehow in that she never had the opportunity to really say goodbye. I'm sure many people feel the same way. There were things she would have said or would have been best to have said. She asked for my advice and my answer was simple:

> "When you feel your friend in the room or nearby, or that friend keeps popping into your mind, talk to her. Talk to her just like she was sitting right beside you. Tell her how you feel, tell her the things you wanted to share but never had the opportunity to. Talk to her normally just like you would in casual conversation; nothing has to be contrived and nothing has to be scripted. Just speak authentically, like any friend would speak to another. Believe me, that person will hear you."

Making statements out loud is not only an absolute way to connect but also very cathartic for the person speaking. Start a conversation, be heartfelt and sincere and talk soul to soul and friend to friend. Just because the person has passed on to another dimension doesn't mean they aren't still nearby. They still hear us too. Then, after you speak to that loved one or friend, be silent for a few seconds and you might hear a reply. It won't be their voice but it may be a thought that pops into your mind, sort of like a knowing. It may be just something simple like "Thank you," "I love you too," or "I'm fine, don't worry." Maybe just a simple: "Me too." And don't discount something you think you might have heard or thought that person said. They probably did. Finally, if you don't hear anything the first few times, don't worry about that either for they still hear every word you say to them.

Such an exercise sounds so simplistic but it's very, very healing for the one doing the talking, and it's helpful to the one on the other side too. Although nothing can physically bring them back, once you connect verbally, you have established a connection that just might bring you closer than you ever were before.

It's impossible to speak to someone on the other side with sincerity and have a closed heart. When your heart is open, love just flows out; and love, my friend, is the connector that will link the two of you forever. And remember to keep your eyes open for signs or signals they send. Don't actively look for them, but when something very weird happens, don't dismiss it. If it feels like it might be your friend or loved one, it probably is. Accept that and smile.

Like Jon said to me on November 22, 2019 in expressing the wonder of all this connectedness:

"I am so grateful you are open for me to come to you this way. Geez, nobody I knew on earth had that kind of connection with a parent or even a friend. Who'd believe this? But for me, it's miraculous. It allows me to clear my guilt, to share the love I wasn't able to before and to try to pay you back for all you gave me."

Of course I told Jon that wasn't necessary, and he responded:

"I know it isn't, but I want to. Everyone wants to have an equal and balanced relationship whereby they can receive and give in love. Whether it's romantic love or parent/child love or friendship love. Doesn't matter. You've made that possible for me and I'm so happy and proud that you'll try to help others see that possibility for themselves."

This is a bit of a sidebar but he followed with this and I felt like I had to include it here since it was in context, even though the thought was totally unrelated. Jon knew how I'd write and write quickly to catch everything he said, so he finished with:

"Just thought of something funny. How can kids today do automatic writing like you do if they don't learn cursive? It'll take them a frigging week to print eight pages since it's so painfully slow to print. Ha! Guess they'll type it. Forgot that. Still, not as energy-pure as handwriting where no machine is involved. Back to basics in school.☺"

For those of you who are still not convinced that a real connection is possible, I have a couple of suggestions for you as well. Filling the hole in your heart after a great loss is much easier if you are able to give love or understanding to someone else. Still, pain is pain and the generous spirit of giving to another is only a temporary fix. Some form of contact with the person departed helps with the emptiness. It's like when a good friend or family member moves out of state, is on a lengthy vacation or is estranged for some reason. You will likely be lonely for that person. What helps is hearing their voice on the phone, receiving a thoughtful text or email, or even picking up something that belonged to them. That connection helps. It's the love we have for them that brings them back to our heart.

So, if the loss is your spouse, it sometimes helps to sleep on their side of the bed. If it is a friend or relative where you have an item or piece of clothing that was theirs, holding onto it sometimes brings comfort. With Jon, for example, I took a couple of the t-shirts he slept in and I slept in them after. In fact, one is uber-soft and it's still my favorite sleeping garment. Adding a few more photos to your home helps also. In fact, for a while I kept the huge blow-up poster from Jon's funeral in my laundry room and every time I walked by I talked to my son. It was a happy photo of him so it always made me smile. Don't be afraid to be creative and don't be afraid to do whatever brings you some level of comfort. The key is to feel love when you do whatever it is you decide to do.

Since love touches the soul, in fact love is the language of the soul, it's always the soul-based connection we yearn for. So anything you can do to make yourself feel closer to the person you miss—going to a favorite spot they loved, listening to music that reminds you of them or browsing through photos that touch your heart and make you happy—even for just a minute is worth it.

The Round-Trip Ticket

Long before Jon's death, I realized that this life has a round-trip ticket that goes right along with it; it's just part of the deal. So, leaving at some point—for everyone—has to be expected. Once Jon passed, the shock was undeniable but the reality that he might have really left for good was no surprise at all. That's why treasuring those we love, every moment they are with us is so very important. Remembering that everything is temporary in life helps us appreciate one another just a little bit more. It helps us become more kind and it reminds us to tell those we love how *much* we love them, whenever the thought pops into our mind.

Then, if the pain of loss persists, channel that pain into helping others. Another dear friend of mine lost her only son, an innocent and loving young man, in a tragic, violent incident when her son was only in his twenties. She could have done something to fight domestic abuse or to protest gun violence, but she chose instead to help young people because her son adored helping kids. She turned her pain into giving to others by forming a nonprofit to help some of the most vulnerable youth in our community. I actually believe her son is working side by side with her.

So, give back. Giving to others helps heal the pain you're feeling. Volunteer, donate, attend events that benefit others and give of yourself, or maybe just help a neighbor or friend in need. The more you give, the more quickly healing comes.

God spoke to me again on December 6, 2019 and shared much about what content would be best for this book. I was well on my way to writing it but His direction helped me refine the core message. I know He has blessed this work. He reminded me:

"This is the lesson, Sandy. We never leave those we love. Love binds us eternally.

The strongest loves are the soul mate connections everyone raves about, but any love can do the trick. So loss is impossible in my world. Love is eternal—so a loving soul and souls that love are connected eternally.

"No wonder I never leave all of you. Can you even imagine the depth of my love? Of course not. So you get the idea. Give mothers and fathers, lovers, friends, siblings and spouses hope that they can reconnect with the perfection they saw in the relationship that

ended, even if living with that person may have been challenging. It is no more."

If part of your pain is the great disappointment you felt from the life your loved one lived, there is no reason to hold on to that resentment, disappointment, pain or anger. All that has ended. His or her soul is now headed, once again, on the path to perfection. They feel guilt and sorrow for those they hurt, and they reach out to all of us with an enormous amount of love, trying to make things right no matter how horrible their life might have been. Connectedness helps correct all mistakes and helps souls grow on the other side. Connectedness heals. Connectedness is the way we were meant to help one another, forever and ever.

Chapter 8
MORE PROFOUND MESSAGES FROM THE OTHER SIDE

I n this chapter I'd like to drill down more completely on some of the subjects Jon and others have brought up to me. When I receive each message, I take it at face value, not wondering if what I receive is the complete message or parts of a much larger subject or puzzle. Sometimes I receive information, piece by piece and not always in the right order. So, I'd receive something that really sounded smart and just be grateful. Then years down the road, I'd receive another part of the same message that fit with what I had received before. Only much, much later and in retrospect could I begin to connect the dots. Timing is everything. Like they say, "The teacher comes when the student is ready."

Jon's passing was clearly the catalyst for me to begin to assemble all this material, or more precisely, to put pieces of the puzzle together so I could share it with others. It was also because Jon could help me connect the dots through my additional questions I'd ask him. The answers Jon shares have helped me see how pieces fit with one another and how I could begin to draw more complete conclusions. Then with my darling son's prompting, the communication with you through this book was born.

Love's Role

Because God's work creating this magnificent Universe and all the other Universes that may exist is so massive and complex, there is no way to ever understand everything He's done or how He's done it. My goodness, science is still trying to figure out how bodies work. It is all so intricate and comprehensive that His greatness can't be distilled down to anything simple. Or, can it?

I'm convinced that the core of God's brilliance is something very simple: love. Have you ever noticed why one carpenter's work is good and another's is absolutely magnificent? Sometimes it's more than simple craftsmanship, there's an X factor. The difference is probably the love he or she pours into the creation. The same with art, music or anything we mortals undertake. Since we're created in God's image, I'm sure when He created this earth, His love was evident in every lush leaf in a tropical landscape, in each little feather on a beautiful, colorful bird's wings and in each petal of the most amazingly gorgeous flower. The beauty that surrounds us is deniable and that can only happen with love at the core.

That is why love is at the foundation of this book, how and why we connect with each other here on earth, and how and why we can connect across dimensions. The root of what God wants us to express in our lives is love. And His love for us is the centerpiece in most of His communications. He loves us eternally, more than anyone in the universe could love anyone else, and more than we can even totally imagine. It's all about love.

Our departed loved ones are basking in love right now, and are sending so much love our way that it might be difficult for us to imagine. If you can accept that as a possibility, let's look at how we might return the favor. What do they need from us and how can we help them? As we all know, you can't have a real relationship with anyone else unless it's mutually beneficial. Crossing dimensions is no different.

For decades now, there has been give and take in my relationship with departed souls. When I was transitioning spirits to help them reach the other side, I was totally giving and felt blessed to be able to help them find peace and arrive where they were supposed to go. Then, once messages started coming to me personally, I was totally receiving. Each was a gift of knowledge, of kindness, of love and often, of humor. Only rarely did I deliver a message to someone else from a departed friend or relative who'd passed and requested that. So, I think overall I received much more than I ever gave in the process.

When Jon died, I discovered that we *can* do something to help those "over there" too, besides just delivering a message once in a great while. First, we can listen. When Jon initially called out with confusion and fear, evident in every word I heard, I talked to him to try to bring comfort. When he came to me in my bedroom three days later and asked for help, I tried to help him transition more easily. I believe I did help with that, if nothing else, maybe Jon felt more secure in the process. Then, as the dialogue began to go back and forth more routinely, I realized he needed to cleanse his soul and heal. He needed to say he was sorry and needed to make sure I knew how much he loved me as well as others in his life. Relieving the guilt was a big part of the process Jon was going through, and my being willing to accept his regret and express love, understanding and forgiveness back to him was helpful too. Connection allows us to help one another. I felt less alone and more loved. He felt more at peace and now he could truly see and receive the love I had given him all of his life.

With this new relationship, profound and often brilliant information is delivered to me from my Jon and it's almost always unsolicited. It's just something he wants to share. It may also be because he is supposed to help me deliver pieces to help me put this puzzle together. Every time I hear from him, something insightful is revealed. Once in a while I ask a specific question but that is really only about thirty percent of the time, the balance is Jon just showing up to amaze his mother.

I also believe his work is not finished and that he and I are now supposed to work together. I believe this book is a start. Wouldn't that be nice? Much of the information Jon has shared with me I have known or realized over the last three decades, but the details, the drill-downs, the curious little pockets of information no one would ever think to share, I can now ask. Jon helps shed light on those subjects to the best of his ability. The dialogue between us is continual and extraordinarily enlightened.

When we connect I am absolutely astounded by Jon's wisdom. That phenomenon is so strange to me because Jon was the guy who'd roll his eyes when I mentioned spirituality and would often mockingly call me "woo-woo." Even with his verbal jousting about the subject, he still was someone who went to an astrologer from time to time, loved Long Island Medium—the TV show, and was very superstitious. Jon was a walking conflict while on earth. He had a four-leaf clover on his desk and carried with him a small bag of minerals I had assembled to bring him positive energy in various aspects of his life. This little bag was a tiny leather pouch with very small stones inside: one to fight addiction, one to combat fear, and others to bring abundance and success. Jon loved that gift when it was presented to him on one of his birthdays. Now, my son is actually teaching me. It's absolutely amazing.

All the barriers Jon had formed over his lifetime have been stripped away. Jon's enlightenment is undeniable to me and now I'm able to recognize the evolved soul I first thought I saw when he was born.

As I mentioned before, during Jon's first two years he was the kindest and most loving child I had ever met. Of course I thought I contributed to that because of the way I referred to others in his presence; I would talk up guests who were about to arrive and by the time they walked in the door, Jon was so thrilled to see them that he'd hug them and hug them. But I was wrong. Later I realized that Jon was just born that way. He was wise and loving in a very unpretentious way right from the start. And all through his life he didn't spout theory or preach or even verbalize about love, he just demonstrated it. Now, all of his love and kindness is back again, along with a layer of universal understanding that shocks me.

I hope that those of you who have lost loved ones, who you knew were wonderful, loving people—even though the lives they led may not have always demonstrated that—can now have faith that you were right. They *are* special. They are loving and kind and good. They are who you always thought they were.

Are You Up or Sideways or Where?

Now this was a question that most wouldn't ever think of asking but when I used to look up at the stars at night and try to see beyond them to where Jon might be now, it would feel frightening and not right. Then my dear friend, Shirley, asked me to ask Jon if he was up or sideways or exactly where Heaven was. My precious son explained:

> *"None of those—(it's) all around you. Just at a different frequency or dimension. Hard for people to grasp. A God place but it does touch everything, which is why we can select life pleasures to experience and why feelings are still a part of our soul's clearing."*

Everything Jon has communicated so far about the importance of loving and helping one another, even across dimensions, makes total sense because living in unconditional love is the real goal in life, right? Then, I asked him another question many people probably want to know, at least in his case.

Have You Seen Jesus?

> *"I've not seen him. But it's not important to me. Much work still to do. When I am more pure, I will connect more strongly to Ascended Masters and Saints. Actually in another frequency. My belief was not strong enough and even though I'm enlightened, all that means is I recognize; it doesn't mean I can do."*

Jon went on to explain that it's a love thing and some, even here on earth, are on a totally different frequency and capable of much greater love than he was. Remember in an earlier chapter Jon said that the goal of soul growth is to become so pure in love that we can all "hang with the big dogs"? Those are the Ascended Masters and this more or less explains the level of frequency our souls achieve during growth from one lifetime to another. Eventually we become more like God, more pure and have no more need for growth. On earth, many people shy away from folks who have much higher love frequencies because they don't feel they deserve, on a soul level, to be in such grace. However, those in the same bandwidth gravitate toward others with a bit more insight and power in order to learn and share. Love, I've come to believe, is the core of that power.

I want to clarify here that when I speak about living in more love and living in grace that does not mean being religious, being a religious teacher or scholar, or going to church every day. You know a person can sit in a garage all day long and that doesn't make them a car. It also doesn't mean living a life of being so "nicey-nicey" or so superficially sweet that it makes people question if someone is even real. You know the type. No, this grace, this love state, creates an aura around a person that people can feel when they connect. It might be an instant smile and warmth, something in the eyes, some feeling that a person would just feel when they meet. It's no doubt that everyone seems to love basking in the feeling such people emote.

A great example, as I mentioned briefly before, is the Dalai Lama. His smile is infectious, his eyes mischievous and fun and he is a truly joyful being. That's grace.

Those are the initial signals of soul growth in love. There are many degrees of that, but that is the grace to which I'm referring.

So, when I asked Jon who he sees in the spiritual realm, he said:

> "Actually, angels a lot. We can seek out others, but I haven't. Been mostly self-reflecting, connecting with souls from this life in a comforting way. Getting settled and kind of balanced or grounded, as it were, up here."

Then Jon said,

> "I'm doing more connecting to earth than more up here. Probably 'cause all is so new."

This message came only two months after he had passed.

How Do You Know When I Need You?

My final question during that period about the afterlife was again about the energy-related interconnectedness and how they know over there that we might need them over here. I had become from time to time pathetic with grief; crying and sobbing, it was really tragic. Then it wouldn't be long until my dear son would come. He just knew.

> *"I feel your energy and pain. It's like a little jolt or top or flicker and then I sort of tune you in. Most times I can look around and see my people in a hazy energetic way and when I like blink or focus, I see the experience. Like when you and the kids are together or when they perform or play a sport or when they or anyone has strong feelings about what they're doing. Our life team is all energetically connected, even over here."*

That's why it is so important for everyone to understand that there is still connectedness and there is still love, lots of love between living souls and those who have passed. Then Jon reminded me about his support. He is my anchor and quite often my cheerleader too.

> *"When you are in pain, when you hurt, when you are afraid of tomorrow, talk to me. I will be near watching out for you, until you come home. I will never leave you. I'll be cheering you on from my perch up here."*

He signed off this way:

> *"Go get'em Momma. Your work isn't done yet."*

Chapter 9
WHAT IS HEAVEN LIKE?

Along with some of Jon's insight that I'm sharing, there are other departed souls I cared about who also felt the need to reach out to me and tell me more, much more, about their passing. One of those was my friend Jack.

Jack was one of the most expressive, totally smart and creative men I had ever known, as a friend and later as a professional in my business. He contacted me shortly after his passing to explain everything. Jack left much too soon. He and I had always had an intellectual connection. He was still in his sixties when he died and although we never seriously talked about the afterlife, in fact I'm not sure we ever talked about it at all, I guess he knew somehow that I'd be curious about what he was now experiencing. Jack also knew I'd "get" whatever it was he was about to explain.

Now remember, I didn't ask for Jack to contact me. I wasn't asking questions or researching about the hereafter; this was a totally unsolicited message from a dear friend:

> *"The reason I'm here talking to you is that I am amazed at this place and how everything works. Guess you know much of that, but for some reason I'm compelled to explain or share. And you're the one I'm compelled to share it with. Okay?"*

Well, it certainly was. Jack had been a friend of mine since the seventies. He was a saloon singer, played piano by ear, was a creative genius and was like a brother to me. I think we loved each other too, but not in a romantic or physical way. We later worked together in the advertising business; in fact, I launched his career in that arena. He took off like a rocket. He was always such a smarty and now I couldn't wait to hear whatever it was dear Jack was about to share:

"Well, to start off, when I first got here it was sort of nothing. Dark all around, but peaceful. A glow above me, but nothing happening. Guess I was moving but I didn't feel motion. Then I saw my folks. Instant comfort. They were smiling as I passed by. Didn't go to them, didn't need to—just an instant connection. I went to a place to decompress, I guess. Get over the shock of leaving and the stress of transition. All white. Very healing. Guess you could say there was a sound there, more like white noise. Again, my reaction was to go within and reconnect with myself. I think I used to try to get to that place when I drank. Ha —not close.

"Anyway, don't know how long I was there but feelings (emotions) emerged sort of one at a time. Some I could put a life situation to and some I could not. Pretty soon I was clean, as it were. Maybe that's where people get the 'life passes before you' bit or the judgment day routine. All I can say is it is very cleansing and liberating when it's done.

"When all that was finished, I moved on to what you would call Heaven. More the stereotypical. Saw so many familiar souls floating by—angels, light, love—permeating but no real scenery to speak of. Just a place to, again, decompress or readjust, I think.

"Then, the 'nature on steroids' Heaven. Seems to me everybody would interpret this differently. For some, ocean. For others, gardens. For others, grassy fields. For me it was scenic tropical plant leaves as thick as the width of a finger. Lush, vibrant, unbelievable. I can come back here as often as I wish. I can go to the other Heavenly place or I can go to what I call the healing center.

"This one is interesting. Sort of a movie room, but not really. I can see all my past lifetimes on the earthly plane (including with

you and others) and inside myself. The impurities of my soul and the growth needed. This is where we communicate with other souls up here, souls on earth and plan our futures.

"God gave us free will, you know, and he really meant it. We can decide what else we need for our 'perfect' growth and then organize the group to get us there next time around."

Jack finished this way,

"Boy, one sure lets go of judgment up here. Even for the bad apples. We all play a role in our earthly lives. We pretty much pre-script, and it's so we can develop our higher selves in each lifetime."

Guess that pretty much explains the concept of reincarnation. I went on to ask Jack if he could tell me anything about my life or role.

"Maybe. Maybe that is why I am still connecting with you. You are a truth-teller Sandy, and you have knowledge and insight others may not have. But you also have the ability to simplify and condense messages so lesser developed souls can 'get it'. Guess I'm supposed to share with you for that reason."

So, here I am sharing what I know and have learned over the last thirty years. None of this is intellectual knowledge, it's what I've learned from much wiser souls—all confirming or reconfirming a knowing I seemed to have had for the last four decades.

At one point, my son Jon also shared with me about what Heaven was like to him.

"Momma, this is really something up here. The warmth, the peace, the pure bliss. No wonder when people get a glimpse they want to stay and aren't anxious to head back to all the problems, tensions, bad energy and all of it on earth. I'm not excited about

another trip back, and am glad I don't have to deal with that for a while."

There will be more on reincarnation and the concept of it later. Jon continued.

"Up here it is glorious. Everything I love is all around me. And, I'm not afraid of dogs here. Ha!."

Jon never liked dogs, and was always a little afraid of big ones, terrified in fact, especially when he was quite young, so this comment made me laugh. Ironically, it wasn't an earthly experience that shaped his fear of dogs, at least not in this life's earthly experience. He may have brought that fear with him from a past existence.

Jon continued,

"Everyone is fine. Ray wants a pitch game. Mill is laughing. Grandma Brandy hugs my soul and everyone was so happy to see me. We are all waiting for you too, but it will be a while – in your time."

Jon later explained that these attitudes, energy and emotions are not literal but rather energies he can pick up from those souls he was mentioning. In fact, this is how he clarified all that when I asked if he sees people in bodies:

"No, you see energy. You feel the mass, the smiling, the laughing, the activities are sort of all on a different level, like a different dimension where you can actually experience things in a way but not like here on earth. For example, card playing. No cards up here, but you can gather together and re-live some happy times objectively and with distance. Hard to explain. You don't feel the emotions like on earth, which is why earth is kind of cool. It is just the bad emotions that were a bummer to experience.

"*Laughter, like with Mill, is easy because everything with her energy is joyous. Some are in an active state of joy (like Mill) and seem to delight more, even up here. That is why I said what I said about her.*"

In another message he said, when I asked again about how he was doing up there,

"*Curious are you? It's great. Peaceful. No stress. All love and joy. A clear perspective about all our lives and the state of our souls.*"

When I asked Jon if he was playing golf up there, he replied,

"*Kind of. Not a physical thing here but I was in those surroundings of walking the course and reliving the Phoenix Open experience. One of my BIG ones. So fun. When you get here, you'll see.*"

Jon had played in the Pro-Am in 1999, I think, can't remember the exact year, but Jon loved golf.

Others came to me and talked about similar experiences, some who surprised me. A man, who I still believe was my soul mate and whom I had started dating in 1971 for two or so years, has communicated with me more than once. His name was Burt. About Heaven, he said this:

"*One day we will reconnect and you will feel the extraordinary bliss that is up here in this dimension. Boy, never want to go back, but do miss the contrast so the 'highs' can be felt.*"

The other odd experience connecting Burt and I happened the morning he passed. I hadn't known he died, that he'd dropped dead on the tennis courts in La Costa where he lived. I was told about it several days later. But on the day he died I had a bizarre dream that I was in a church and as

I was moving into the pew, someone put their arms around my waist to hug me. The feeling was so strong that it woke me up. I continued to feel those arms around me as I walked around my bedroom. I was actually frightened and had no idea what it meant. Days later I found out that Burt had died that very day, and I honestly believe he came to say goodbye to me with that hug.

Burt didn't stop with those experiences or messages. While I was struggling with whether to just do a complete book on Heaven, he came to me and offered to send others to me to give their perspective. This is precisely what he said,

> *"I'll ask people to contact you who already haven't; some challenged and struggling, so a cross-section. So glad I can help. Include that mention somewhere! Ha"*

I told him I'd quote him and he burst out laughing. Kept my promise.

So Many Voices, Such Similar Messages

The first of Burt's referrals was the husband of Marcia, whom I quoted earlier. Marcia was the gorgeous woman who always wore the same shoes as I did, or vice versa. Her husband, Mal, was a pillar in the community, had a kind heart and everyone loved him —that is until the end.

> *"Isn't it great? Who'd have thought? Really glad Burt made this happen. I guess I'm supposed to talk about my experience here. So here goes."*

Mal went on to explain the circumstances surrounding the ongoing relationship that broke his wife's heart, thus contributing to the sudden illness that took her too soon. How we can subconsciously speed up our demise is another story; too long to explain here but suffice it to say that giving up and wanting out are powerful emotions that when felt at the soul level stick. Mal continued:

"*Regrets and guilt. Yep, punished myself for hurting my beauti-ful little girl* (his wife Marcia). *The pain of feeling what Marcia felt, magnified. The pain of feeling the humiliation of knowing everyone knew and many hated me was also rough. Then, my own guilt. Layer that stuff one on the other and I finally think I bal-anced the scale.*

"*I didn't have a deep enough concern for other's true feelings—only in a superficial way there. So now I realize how selfish actions can more than devastate those we love. That deal was the worst thing I ever did.*

"*But the joy part of Heaven for me is realizing how many spe-cial, truly special souls exist up here. Never thought much about what or whom other religions worshipped, but they are all here. And nobodies who should have been recognized too, but who lived to show others how to live lifetime after lifetime, are here and their souls shine as brightly as the names everyone knows.*

BTW, Marcia forgave me the moment I got here. Never anger. Anyway, just hurt and that was the worst—Jewish guilt."

When I asked him what his joyful experience in Heaven is like, he told me,

"*The ocean. On boats—sail or motor—or just sitting on the beach. The smell of salt water, the sun reflecting on the waves and water's surface. I loved the ocean.*"

I could hear the love in his voice,

"*But I'm so content here now, and a bit tired. Not sure if I come back or not. Hasn't come up yet. My soul needs rest and healing. Don't think I had a ton to learn this time. I was just there to do my thing and obviously be a catalyst for Marcia's exit. Hated that the most. Not sure I'd have done things any differently, but even if we are fairly innocent with the wrongs we do and the hurts we cause, we still relive them to learn or to do our penance for being stupid. Ha! That's fair. Small stuff, not so much. But big stuff, absolutely !!"*

Finally Mal concluded,

"Let people know to never be afraid of death. It isn't an ending, it's just a moving on. Soul relationships continue forever. I'm now here with Coke and Bill and Marcia and Burt and Barry (Goldwater) and the gang. Great! Thank you for being there Sandy, and for being interested. This will help others, I know it! Much love, Mal."

Another Prominent Voice

I was surprised by Burt's next referral. This man, a prominent jeweler in town for decades, was on the Phoenix City Council when it was a powerful body in the fifties, and was head of the Republican Party during the fifties and sixties. He was a close friend of Barry Goldwater and a local legend. He was also one of the most powerful men in Phoenix at the time. I knew Harry casually, but we weren't as close as Mal, Marcia, Burt and I. Anyway, I was shocked when all sorts of electrical commotions got my attention:

"Sandy, do you remember me? It's good to connect again. Seems different from here but it's the best way for souls to communicate, independent of life's experiences, more time, more meaningfully. Don't you think? Burt asked me to come and I'm thrilled to help. Do you want to know about Heaven, or what?"

It's amazing how loving and open the souls are when they connect with us, willing to help in any way. So I asked if he would first share about love.

"*Of course. Love. That's all there is. We wise old guys during our lifetimes were always chasing beautiful young women. Do you think that was all about sex? No !! It was about love. Receiving it, basking in it, bathing in it. Ha! That's why we showered our girlfriends with presents—to feel the gratitude and love. We weren't dummies and none of us were sexual animals. It was all about relationships with youth and beauty and vitality and love. Our girlfriends were always working—probably twenty-five to thirty year olds—so no pedophile stuff; pure, really. And now look where I am? Up here with beautiful angels who shower me with music, song and gentle breezes from their wings and beauty! My!! It's amazing.*"

I guess Harry, without knowing it, also answered the question that would come later about how his passions would come alive in Heaven. Mal's was the ocean. Harry's must have been beautiful women.

"*I had a wonderful life Sandy. And, I always tried to help women, mainly women I had known or those of my friends. I don't think we were crude then, just silly old guys who didn't want to age. So, to your love question, I always sought it. So now, as you'd say, I'm in Heaven.*"

I continued to ask him about his death and transition. He replied,

"*When I died I realized right away what was happening to me and I surrendered. I always believed in God and feared Him in a way—feared that he'd know who I was inside—imperfect, for sure. But my love for Him was stronger than my fear. No particular challenge in ascending.*

"*I saw flashes of those I knew welcoming me. I was guided also by my family, who had passed and those who were the most loving came for that process. Then I rested in beauty until the shock wore off. Pure beauty—glistening, opaque surroundings like those paintings by Andrew Wyeth. Just the sky parts with gold light and white glow coming through the softness.*

"I decompressed from the initial feelings of sadness, longing, shock, regret, guilt— those quick flashes that come to you when you realize it's the end. When I was finally at peace, I was ushered into my life room where I flashed back to all the life experiences where I had intense feelings that stuck with me. Some of those do, you know.

"With some, I felt the intense joy and with others the pain. The painful ones were the ones that stayed in my vision until I had completed ridding my soul of the feeling, either through sorrow and forgiveness of self to release, or until others came to explain the gift to me so I could release. There are always gifts in these impactful life experiences. Character building, gifts to others, course correction or payback for earlier Karmic experiences.

"The reality helps cleanse, so does forgiveness. Then gratitude can follow and that is the love space we are all in up here. Eternal gratitude, but it is not as tight and specific and defined as it is more a 'state of being' instead of a state of mind. Bliss, really.

"I also have my personal Heavenly experiences," he added.

Okay, now I was really shocked. I thought it was the women, but nope. Harry had other ideas about Heaven.

"Big dinners and events and galas; beautiful people, wonderful food, great speakers, experiences of an elevated kind with much beauty and ceremony. Anything like that. People all around. I loved people. I loved beauty and I loved wisdom."

Harry went on to lecture me about my life, as he observes it from over there. And he was curious about why I hide my power and wisdom under some sort of bushel barrel. I laughed. He wondered why I was timid and didn't seem to realize whom I attract. Of course Harry knew of the political figure who had noticed me and had come in an earlier message. Harry mentioned him by name. Then he quipped,

> *"It's time kiddo. You're not getting any younger. ☺ Bring back wisdom to the older generations. Stay beautiful and wise and articulate and help bring people home to love, and therefore to God."*

He acknowledged my son and that touched my heart.

> *"Jon is here and he has your spark. He is wise too. We all love his energy—a matched set. ☺ ☺"*

There was more in this rather lengthy but wonderfully welcome contact with a man I had always admired and adored. Harry was always a sweetie pie.

A More Troubled Soul Arrives in Heaven

The final person from Burt's tribe was his son, Rick. Rick had a tragic life and therefore I felt it made sense to hear, in-depth, about what it's like when a soul that is totally lost on the earth makes the transition. His was a different story.

"I was a mess. My life was a mess. I died of AIDS-related causes from bad needles. I was, among other things, a heroin addict. Dad was with me, as was Mom, when I died. I died in the hospital. I knew I was dying, so I wasn't confused when I left.

"Family, several, greeted me or rather ushered me through the process. It was transformative, really. I could feel the transition and things (my world) got more narrow and definitely better.

"I too went through a reflective state, and boy, it was an experience to do real soul searching. I was selfish, spoiled, ignorant about life and absent of very many values. I was raised by a dad who loved me, I guess, but he was also selfish and not strong emotionally. Only in business was he strong and that was confusing to me. My mom was spoiled and selfish and

although they did the best they could, it wasn't a very healthy environment for me. Not complaining, I picked it. ☺

"*Here, I saw how other people's lives were happier and more rich, and mainly through caring for others besides themselves. Helping others in one way or another. I never did any of that. I liked Jackie* (his Dad's last wife) *and she was sweet to me, but I was lost.*

"*I don't reach out to anyone* (from up here), *really. Dad helped me with finding you. Not sure what I'd say. I have so much to learn, and don't think I am a very mature soul or else I'm a very slow learner. I do experience joy up here but for me it comes in the form of emotional peace, like being wrapped in a nice soft blanket, snuggling in. Actually it's the place I really wanted to find through drugs. Who'd have known that finding God would have helped me in that life. Oh, well.*

"*Here, the love is so overwhelming that dummies like me are just shocked into a state of wonderment and gratitude for the experience. I didn't do anything like a punishment thing. Believe I had enough of that while alive—conning, stealing, lying.*

"*Again, I was a mess. Drugs were my God and it's hard to live when one knows they are a continual disappointment to those they love. But all is good here.*"

Rick volunteered his passion, in the form of Heavenly experience, without asking.

In fact, his message was one long one, with no breaks at all.

"*I love music and experience the depths and richness of sounds you could never fathom.*

"*Anyway, I'm at peace. Haven't made a plan to come back. I'm not even sure which part of my screwed up existence I'd work on, so any of my tribe will likely drag me back in some role and I'll learn what I need by accident. Ha, guess I'll be back a lot.*

"*That's okay. Up here one isn't afraid of a thing, so <u>whatever</u> works for me.*

"I hope this helps you Sandy. My dad sure loved you. Guess you two had some sort of connection. You seem nice, so I'll bet I'd have liked you too. And, you're pretty. That was a must for my dad. Ha! Will be signing off now. Fondly, Rick."

All souls are so different, each with their own story. Some babies in the process and still a little lost, others more experienced and enlightened. It's the innocent ones that tug at my heart.

Family Speaks Up Next

Others have shared a glimpse of heaven, and a special one among them was my half-brother, Gary. Later in my life, I met my birth mother and found I also had four half-sibblings. Gary was the oldest and he has since passed. He was an evangelical Christian, quite devout and an absolute angel of a man. I adored him. Not long after his death, he contacted me in a not too subtle way—a florescent light exploded and fell out of the socket. He had a lot to say, but this was the most relevant part for this chapter:

"Sandy, it is glorious here. This is a glorious dimension, not a place, and it oozes with love and peace and light. The perfect environment for soul healing."

Other More Surprising Voices

Two others came to me and were big surprises as well. They were the parents of a dear friend of mine, Peter, whom I dated in the seventies briefly, then reconnected with on a "fix-up" in the early 2000's and we dated again for a few years. We remain close to this day.

Peter had a privileged life, well, more than privileged. He was from one of the most prominent families in the country throughout the twentieth century—the du Pont family. Originally the du Ponts were a French family whose DuPont company and all its subsidiaries in those years constituted a fortune. Peter wasn't some remote connection to that family, his grandfather had married a du Pont sister and sat on the board of DuPont Chemical for decades and was instrumental in its diversification from the explosives industry to the chemical one. Therefore, Peter's last name was not du Pont.

Anyway, Peter's father had passed prior to me ever meeting him but I was fortunate to meet his mother, Francis (yes, she spelled it with an "i" instead of an "e") and she was really something. She and Billy (Peter's father), while they were still married, made many trips to Africa. Both Francis and Billy were enamored with wild animals; Francis would adopt one or two and Billy would shoot the others. Billy was a big-game hunter and world-class fisherman, and the stories from their lives could fill volumes.

Anyway, both their spirits came to me over a period of a year to ask me to communicate with their son. And, in the course of those messages both spoke about Heaven. Peter said they wouldn't mind me sharing this. His mother, Francis came first:

I'm happy up here. Lots of beauty in which I thrive and lots of beautiful people. ☺" *"Oh, and there are animals here. The most magnificent creatures I could ever imagine. Yes, I guess I am in Heaven."*

Francis was a woman who only loved beautiful people and things. Her home was all in pastels and if anyone sent her flowers, the florists in Nantucket and in Palm Beach knew to never send her bold or primary colors—only pastels. Francis was one-of-a kind.

When Billy, Peter's father, came through, it was easy to see that one's passions in life can easily show up on the other side to be enjoyed limitlessly. This man spent his life hunting, fishing, flying and navigating the world on his incredible yacht. Nature was his passion. This was a portion of the message he wanted to me to convey to his son:

"No fishing or hunting up here but I am surrounded by the most magnificent creatures God ever created, the current and the extinct. My idea of Heaven, absolutely."

Finally, I'll let my friend Jack help bring this section about Heaven to a close since I found one more message from him that was fascinating. In one later message, Jack communicated:

"Interesting, warm and loving brings out the best in us spirits. ☺ Really something. Holograms, depth, beauty like nature on steroids. But I think really the most impressive is the warmth and resounding love that permeates everything. Family and friends pass in and out, but it doesn't matter. We here are one with God in a most grand way. I guess I never really realized how special I was, how special we all are."

Jack continued, after having jumped around to another couple of topics.

"Like I was saying, guess I've never been so at peace and I am able to look at life like a big picture. No trees here, just forest. Can be objective and love myself even when I was less than lovable."

He wrapped it up by saying,

"Can't wait for you to get here. Oh, sorry !!!"

And ended with a smile. That was Jack.
The final closeout, of course, will come from my son.

"I'm good. It's Heaven here! ☺ Actually, bliss is pretty hard to describe but just becomes a 'state'. Down there the downs are lousy but it makes you appreciate the ups. Really, earth is a terrific experience even though I drew the short straw this time around."

Jon's life this time was really challenging for him, and I knew that somehow. Jon always tried, I saw it, especially in the last two years of his life. He was amazingly resilient, going back time and time again to restart his career in a field where everyone knew his history. He was desperate to be a good father and a good former husband; his intentions were pure, his choices were just horrible. Not sure he really had that much control about those choices one I understood the few tools he had to use in the path his life was to take this time around.

Although I didn't understand that much about karma or how that all works, my son explained it to me. Some believe karma is only punishment but that is not so. Sometimes karma is for learning from an experience or experiences so one can find the right path the second or third time. So, Jon's last quote in this chapter, *"Really, earth is a terrific experience even though I drew the short straw this time around,"* is the perfect segue to what we'll chat about next.

Chapter 10
KARMA AND REINCARNATION ...
HMMM

The reason karma and reincarnation are being mentioned here is that Jon made several references to karma in his earliest messages to me. I knew a little about karma, or thought I did, but certainly nothing compared to hearing directly from someone who explains his karma experience after the fact.

Reincarnation is a bit different, related but still a different subject; it is much more controversial and a subject on which many people disagree. Karma, at least the term, is much more routinely used and has been in the popular vernacular for some time.

Common usage typically refers to getting back a dose of what you've dished out, with the most common phrase being "Karma is a bitch!"

So, let's take a look at both karma and reincarnation and see if there is any common ground based on the perspective of those who have paid the piper and are now in a state of reflection. So far, I only know one such soul but perhaps more will decide to contact me in the future.

On the subject of reincarnation, I'm not here to persuade any reader one way or the other, I'm just here to share what has been told to me from a number of souls who've passed on, Jon being one of them. Jon's comments on this subject were extraordinarily personal, but I assure you he wants me to share exactly what he said about the karma he endured, why that experience was important to his "learning" and why he's so glad this lifetime is over.

Through all Jon's messages to me, he's said over and over that nothing I could write about him or repeat from what he's communicated would be off-limits. He wants me to share with others whatever it takes to help people understand what life's journey is really about, how to make their transitioning into the afterlife easier and how to live a more peaceful and joyful life while on earth. Jon wants me to quote him, wants me to share anything that might be relevant, and hopes in that way his life can make a lasting and meaningful contribution to many.

Those of you who may think I am sharing too much in this chapter, or too many personal details of my son's life, don't know Jon. Jon wouldn't let me get too far astray since I believe he hovers around while I'm writing (I think) and he'd simply blow up my computer if I wandered too far afield.

When Jon was born, as I said before, I knew he was something special. Sounds like every mother, right? No, I had a critical eye and very high standards. This little guy seemed amazing to me from the moment I first saw him in the delivery room. But in his adult life, Jon was anything but wise and insightful. He was just another human being with all the flaws and weaknesses we all have; albeit some of Jon's were a bit exaggerated. So when Jon came to me after his passing to share something I thought was particularly enlightened, I'd comment on my amazement and he'd just laugh.

> *"I told you I was an enlightened soul, you could have told that in my eyes—that first baby picture of me in the incubator thing. I was checking it all out. I was ready. Fortunately for me, I'd forgotten what this life's journey was going to contain or I wouldn't have been so wide-eyed. I'd be squinting with those eyes tightly shut and a grimace on my face. 'Oh, no—here it comes!!' I'd have thought! ☺☺"*

Although Jon had mentioned karma to me quite quickly after his passing, it wasn't until six weeks later, August 21, 2018, when I received a long message from him at which time I asked Jon about what karma had to do with his life. I wanted more clarity.

"I can tell you in past lives I was very judgmental. I thought I was 'hot shit', looked down on others, had no empathy or compassion for their struggles. And you my dear mother, agreed to put up with all this crap from me in this lifetime."

Jon's reference about me agreeing to put up with his life journey this time is based on what I had ascertained for several decades about how a team of souls pulls together on the other side to create a life experience in which they can all learn, or support one another in learning. This does not leave God out of the equation for it was God who gave us complete free will and free will has no limitations. Plus, God orchestrates all the complexity of the process, how every aspect works together like the conductor in the most amazing and complex symphony ever. Therefore, the process of that team effort and how it benefits everyone is so amazingly intricate that it's impossible to explain.

The same souls seem to gravitate toward one another (a tribe, you might call them) on the other side and return lifetime after lifetime, generally in much different roles. It's not necessarily a small group, so some lag back deferring, and some idiots sign up for the really difficult stuff. But the benefits for those participating are huge in terms of the eventual soul growth. Such growth occurs for both the learner and the helpers.

I obviously signed up to help Jon with this life. Later I found out I signed up to help others too, some in very painful ways. Boy, I wasn't paying attention when that sign-up sheet was passed around, probably distracted by the beautiful harp music. Anyway, the experience with Jon was the most amazing for me, regardless of how challenging the assignment might have been for nearly thirty years. The joy he brought me from just seeing his smile was worth everything and anything else. I don't believe that I've ever loved anyone as much as I loved (and love) the one constant in my life, my son.

I guess Jon was giving me an attagirl when he continued,

"You have no idea how powerful your role was in this life. Going through BS so others could learn their lessons. The good news is

that in doing so, you also learned profound lessons in life that, through your gifts of synthesizing, simplifying, clarifying and translating, you could communicate these lessons to others.

Health, emotions, parenting, nonjudgmental living, spirituality. I think you are a Master Teacher, Momma, and isn't it ironic that I am the one closest to you and the one person who never would listen to your sound wisdom and practical advice. What a schmuck!"

I could see his smile, the perfect punctuation for that sentence. Jon went on, as I quoted earlier:

"My life this time was to learn what it feels like and how powerless it is to be a total fuckup! However, my heart was good. I tried and did have a pretty funny sense of humor. So, all was not lost."

That was Jon's life in a nutshell. He was charming, quick-witted, handsome and had a smile that dazzled. Perfect for commercial real estate. Plus, he loved people and people could feel his caring; he was great at client service. Jon had an amazingly impressive future ahead of him, until the effects of addiction began to take a toll.

Over the years, too much alcohol affects one's judgment. Not just when drinking, but in general. Jon began drinking at around fifteen, I think. When opioids were introduced into his life two decades later, they became even more devastating. It was then that drugs become the focus—not work, not responsibility, not much of anything. Jon's children were the exception but even that effort was compromised by his waning financial ability. It's a challenge when you can't afford to take your children to dinner, even a fast-food restaurant, and they hate hanging out in your dark, depressing apartment. Anyway, an obvious problem. Addiction is a mess.

All this was particularly tragic for someone like Jon, who knew what success early in life looked and felt like. His first $500,000 commission check happened when he was around thirty, which was almost twenty years before he passed. Jon knew how one's finances could dramatically change with one big deal, but tragically his real issue had nothing to do with money, although he thought it did. And sadly the "one big deal" would not happen again on the path Jon had chosen. He went on to describe how he was seeing his life in retrospect.

"You were right in the beginning when you thought I was just given to you to care for."

As you remember, I shared earlier how I never had that funny possessiveness over my child as some parents do. The "my blood, my lineage" thing seemed ego-driven to me and I couldn't connect to it. I knew Jon's soul was independent of mine, even though he was my son. I also knew he was a gift to me to cherish and care for, only. As his mother, I was always there to help and I tried to be there for him. But Jon distanced himself from me when he wanted to hide how he was living his life. I think he knew I could see right through him.

"I never relied on you, like most kids do. I never asked for help or brought people by to stay close-knit. This life was my lesson, and frankly your help only would have slowed down the process (of growth) for me."

Part of Jon's guilt, after passing, was that I had to experience the many years prior and witness the parts of his life he ended up hating. He knew it was painful for a mother to watch when she could do nothing to help. Once a man is in his thirties and forties his life is totally his own. He doesn't need or want his mother preaching to him or giving him unsolicited advice. I was told that repeatedly when I tried to speak up.

So, I was happy to remain at arms length, peeking in once in a while to make sure he was basically okay, that his relationship with his family was good (he adored his three children and nothing brought him more joy than being with them). His former wife was wonderful in that regard, never keeping the kids from Jon, except right after rehab when his addiction had been labeled and she had made sure the children received counseling and that I supervised their visits with Jon for a period. That was particularly kind to me and I am forever grateful. I think deep inside they both always loved each other; it was just a difficult deal for both of them all around.

Jon continued to talk to me and I could feel his sorrow.

> *"I don't know how to make up for how I treated you and how I left* (meaning how he died) *and all the disappointments along the way. I was dealt a lousy hand. I tried my best, I really did. I was just ill-equipped."* He closed by saying, *"I'm doing more soul growth up here."*

Not all lives are karmic experiences. Sometimes karma is just one pure experience someone has to endure in their lifetime on earth to hopefully teach them a lesson. For others it is an entire lifetime so they learn, through submersion in the experience, what they were too ignorant to see in a past life or lifetimes. Unfortunately, the latter was Jon's fate.

He told me later that the Good Lord snatched him out in the nick of time, since there was no recovering from the last stumble on his path of addiction. There were no financial resources left from either of us to get him into rehab. His children would likely have never forgiven this setback. His career couldn't have stood a third bite at the apple (in attempting yet another comeback) and all his credibility with friends had already been stretched to the limits. When he screwed up this last time, it was really a screwup. God saved him, big-time.

The good news is that once Jon was in a reflective state, on the other side, he saw the good in his life, and of course the one thing he was most proud of was his children, Charlie, Jack and Lucy, and the experiences he was able to share with them. His heart was always a hundred percent with those kids, always. Leaving his children was the most painful experience of all, and why his first thought was for a "do-over."

He was so shocked that he had died, he couldn't understand. He used poor judgment buying street drugs that were laced with fentanyl, which killed him. He was totally ignorant and then he was dead. The mulligan he wanted wasn't going to happen and no one could possibly know how painful it was for me to hear that process evolve, but throughout that day or so there was also no question how much Jon adored his precious three children and me.

"I'm sorting everything out up here though and I think I learned in this life what I was supposed to learn. Saw it right away when I arrived (in Heaven)*. Well, not right that minute—but within a bit. I knew the karma lesson and was able to appreciate the lesson, so I recognized how I had been* (in past lives) *and knew I was different now.*

"I really was a good friend to everyone who was hurting or afraid. I sympathized with them. I was patient with them and I didn't judge. I was fair. So, I think I did okay and am not hard on myself in that regard. Where I am hard on myself and where I feel the worst is how I treated you my entire life. I didn't appreciate you. I loved you in my core, but I couldn't see who you were. The reason I think is because you would have helped me, had I recognized your amazing talent, your compassion and your love for me. It would have been your life, not mine 'cause you would have solved the problems and made it easier for me. That isn't what was supposed to happen. Still, I am so very sorry I hurt you. But, Momma, I know you knew I loved you and I know that you held on to the little tiny crumbs I gave you. Amazing. Now, I am here for you for the rest of your life, and then beyond. ☺ ☺ ☺"

Guilt. Get Rid of it Before You Leave Earth

Guilt must be important to alleviate for soul growth because Jon has petitioned over and over for forgiveness and expressed sorrow and contrition. From the first mention, I've told him it was okay and that I loved him unconditionally and forever. That wasn't enough. Guilt is something a person feels themselves, nobody can give it to you (except Catholic and Jewish mothers) and nobody can remove it. Whether we are astute enough to rid ourselves of that guilt while we are still on earth or we wait to do so from the other side, it's important to do it.

Guilt is another reason why connecting with souls who have passed is so very powerful. I know Jon's realization of his growth on the other side was rapid because he was able to express himself, experience the soul cleansing of any guilt he felt, and also to help the injured party on earth heal as well. The power of making amends to those you injured is unquestionable.

In all of the messages from Jon over the first years, the majority of each one dealt with how sorry he was for causing me worry and pain in life and for making a stupid mistake at the end that forced his departure and resulted in my pain in finding him. I was the one Jon was the most hard on, probably because I am the one who knew him best. But, he also felt tremendous guilt and sadness for leaving his children without a father.

So, when souls connect with us, it's very often to help them cleanse more quickly, to have an outlet for expressing their guilt and regret, and for trying to make true amends.

On Saturday, July 21, 2019, Jon expressed that guilt and sorrow for causing me pain. Messages like this came over and over again when he would see me in a pathetic lump, crying about losing him.

> *"Momma, don't cry. I thought the TV would get your attention and you'd smile."*

Jon signaled me by screwing up my TV channels, which always used to happen by itself and then I'd have to call Jon into my room to help me fix them. He'd laugh since technology and I aren't the best of friends. However, since he left the channels have worked perfectly—until now.

> *"Oh, please don't be so heartbroken. Please. I love you so very much and am so sorry I had to leave. It was my time, I guess. I just didn't expect it and I am so sorry you had to find me like that."*

Over and over, Jon tried to make me feel better and came to me when I truly needed him even when I was doing fairly well, just to say how sorry he was for any pain he caused me, ever. Jon always had a kind heart as a child and for everyone he met in his adult life especially his friends and children. That never changed.

A perfect example of that is when Steve and I first told him I had been diagnosed with leukemia in 1999. He looked stunned and the first thing he said was he'd volunteer for any kind of transplant or anything I needed. Jon was a real heart. But with me, it was primarily during critical times when I saw that deep love. Well, sometimes when he'd walk by and pat me on the fanny—those experiences were very endearing and I knew how much he truly loved me. Or at holidays and when his children were around, he then was so happy, and he'd smile that remarkable smile at me. I knew the smile was filled with love. But most other times I couldn't find that heart of his anywhere.

"Oh, my Momma. I feel your pain tonight and am so sorry that I hurt you so throughout my life. No one could have loved me more or did love me more than you. Please let me make it up to you from here."

I smiled because Jon was being so very kind. I also told him he didn't have to do anything.

"I know. I know. And I am so sorry. And I am so sorry. You were the most beautiful and smartest and most wonderful mom. Creative and fun and full of adventure and life. You forced growth from everyone around you. Me, the most. I owe anything good that I was to you."

Messages like that were constant for over the first year. He was truly, truly sorry and his guilt had nothing to do with any demands from me, or what I expected or even what I may have longed for. He looked at his life and he knew how he had behaved with me. Nobody had to say a word. I loved him my entire life, unconditionally, and he was aware of that too. He continued:

> *"Momma, you're brilliant and I see you glow from here. Please don't be brokenhearted over me. I am so sorry. I will tell you that every day of your life, if it will help. I'll do anything to make this right. Oh Momma, please quit sobbing. I am so deeply sorry. You have done so well until now. I can't imagine the pain and shock of finding me. Oh, I am so sorry. I am so sorry."*

Jon has always continued to express regret and sorrow, but much less frequently now. I am adjusting and he has cleared much of his guilt, I believe. But, he still watches over and talks to me about how much he adores his children and is so sorry to have left them. Those messages though are private and are between them and their father, when they are ready and able to accept all this information.

Expressing guilt and cleansing is also a part of a karmic release and purifying, I believe. But, I think the overall lesson on karma is that it is rarely punishment. It's a choice we make to learn and grow through experiences that help us do that. Because those experiences may have been related to past life errors in judgment, or the hurt we caused others is typically the reason, but it is not to punish ourselves. It is to understand at a deeper level.

It is our choice to experience karma. Jon chose this life and I chose to help him with it. Doesn't mean he wasn't thrilled when the pain of it was over, but his soul grew enormously through the experience.

Soul growth is so we become more pure in love energy and let the fearful, negative and angry energy fall away. Love energy raises our vibration or frequency and helps us become more like our Divine Creator, the ultimate goal. Being created in His image means there are big shoes to fill. We all want to be more like Him and since none of us come here with a perfect soul, fixing all that might take more than one go-around.

Reincarnation in Religious Teaching

We can look at the concept of reincarnation as it's communicated through religious teachings. Let's begin with Christianity and Judaism, where in mainstream thinking it is either ignored or totally dismissed as nonsense. I believe that Islam totally rejects the concept with no caveat. However, particular groups within both Christianity and Judaism do refer to reincarnation in their teachings, such as the mainstream historical and contemporary followers of Cathars, Alawites, the Druze and the Rosicrucians.[5] I can add to that list those who study Kabbalah, a more mystical form of Judaism. Kabbalah does teach that reincarnation is not a punishment for sin or a reward for virtue, instead they believe the Jewish soul is reincarnated enough times only in order to fulfill each of the 613 *mitzvahs,* or commandments to be obeyed.[6] Another dear friend of mine, a devout Orthodox Jew, told me that Jews, at least in his circles, do believe that reincarnation is a reality.

The source for dismissal from most people is the Bible itself. Yet, when I looked at the reference section of a study Bible, I found there is no such word as reincarnation within the text of the Bible. Of course, I'm not sure back then they didn't use that word to describe returning again. Still, I looked for anything that might reference that concept. Only these seemed curious to me:

> "As he went along he saw a man blind from birth. His disciples asked him, 'Rabbi, who sinned, this man or his parents, that he was born blind?'" (John 9:1-2)

Someone might interpret this as if a man was being punished for his own sin and was born blind, it must have been from a previous life.

Another says:

> "Naked I came from my mother's womb, and naked I shall return there." (Job 1:21)

The question being, how can a man return to his mother's womb if not through rebirth into another body? Again, always a matter of interpretation. References in the Bible have been debated by religious scholars for 2,000 years, contributing to the different religions that have formed throughout those millennia.

I am no religious scholar and profess little knowledge of the Bible, but I will share what I have studied and have an opinion about. When I was reading about Jesus' early life as a practicing Jew, various sources indicated that the young Jesus went to study with the Essenes, a sect of Jews to which his mother, Mary, belonged. Jesus sought to learn all he could about God as well as life itself in his earlier journeys and studies. He learned from the rabbis at various temples, he learned from men and women he met, from life he experienced and directly, of course, from his Heavenly Father. Yet, I believe though others may ignore this fact, Jesus was not a stranger to what and who the Essenes were.

The Essenes were an interesting group. I encourage even fundamental Christians to read more about them even though they were ignored historically. The Gospels never mention the Essenes. The rabbis seem to have forgotten about them. I believe the Essenes were marginalized by omission. Yet, it seems obvious that Jesus studied as a boy with this group, since the Essenes were his mother's people and it is impossible to think they had no influence on Jesus' early spiritual growth.

The Essenes were given to the study of "mysteries" and the pursuit of esoteric practices, healings and various forms of divination. Simply stated, the Essenes believed in the immortality of the soul and that they would receive their souls back after death.[7] Some of the most elaborate and detailed esoteric representation of the Essenes comes from the Edgar Cayce readings, performed between 1934 and 1945. Cayce was one of the most famous mediums or psychics to receive information from beyond. His teachings on healing have been embraced and practiced by thousands and perhaps millions of healthcare providers and patients worldwide. Yet, back to the subject of reincarnation, Cayce writes that the Essenes would include astrology, numerology, phrenology and phases of study of the return of individuals or incarnation in their scope of interest.

With that said, in all the teachings from Jesus, I don't see any reference that speaks for or against reincarnation. If Jesus was so averse to the subject, it seems to me there would have been a reference refuting the concept, yet the subject only seems to have been ignored. I would question whether that might be a matter of scholarly omission in translation or interpretation.

Okay, I realize some of my readers were traumatized by that thought. But if a person is truly open-minded, seems like an honest question. Anyway, we can all accept this as fact. Some people believe in the existence of reincarnation, the concept of coming back to perfect one's soul, and some do not. Believing in reincarnation or not has nothing to do with souls still being able to love us from afar, reach out to us and even, yes, communicate with us. So, just ignore any references to what I might introduce on the subject of reincarnation if it offends you, otherwise you'll miss the much richer part of the overall message: our loved ones are not that far away and they still love us.

My son wrapped up his references to returning or not returning this way. When I asked him on one visit, how he was doing he said:

> "Great. Not planning a return trip back there for a while! The last one was a doozy. So glad it's over. And, now I see the kids will be fine. I now they realize how much I loved them." As he continually references to me, he is always watching over them, always proudly.

Over decades of being exposed to many religions, experiencing a handful personally, and being open and tolerant of most beliefs, I have come to know a few things to be absolutely true. God gave us all free will. That was unconditional, which means we have the power to reflect on our lives, make our own judgments, and realize where growth is needed—here or elsewhere. And I just happen to believe that we can return to refine ourselves, if we wish.

Secondly, God wanted us to always love each other unconditionally and help one another. Not sure, as I said before, that those relationships had to remain only horizontal.

Again, the concept of soul growth makes perfect sense to me. Once we ascend and see how our soul is progressing in becoming more like God (full of unconditional love for all), we also can judge the flaws and the areas for improvement that still exist. How we fix those, I guess, is still open to debate. But I also believe we are truly our harshest judges. God is loving and kind. So, although many of us were and are taught in our religions that God will punish us for our sins, it seems contradictory for God to be loving and kind, and at the same time judgmental and punitive. He might be disappointed. He might be hurt. But, I can't believe He wields His wrath on the children He loves. Wielding wrath is a human trait not a God-like one.

There is no question that once a soul reaches Heaven, God's love surrounds them.

It's the judging part that remains a bit of a question.

What is Hell Like?

This lesson for me was a private one. It didn't come from speaking to Jon or from receiving guidance from the other side, directly. The lesson came in a dream, the most impactful dream I've ever had in my life. That dream occurred sometime around 2004, when I was living on Exeter Boulevard in Scottsdale. I wrote a blog about it titled *Hell: The Fire and Brimstone Myth."* I think that blog is worth sharing:

> Devils with pitch forks, little men in red suits with tails, burning fire and eternal pain never made much sense to me since we come from a compassionate, loving God. But, I also never gave much thought to what punishment on the other side might really look like either. Although lots of books and articles are written about what heaven may be like, I don't think I've ever seen much, if anything, about what hell might really be like.
>
> Then about eight years ago I had a dream. It wasn't your normal dream. It was one hell of a dream. It was emotionally wrenching, full of fear and guilt and so intense that I was totally

stunned by the depth of the emotional pain it generated. When I awoke, I still felt the anguish.

Let me try to explain the subject matter. The images that still stuck with me were that of a single mother (me) with a young son (mine – about four) in the midst of an orgy of bodies. Jon was not with me, but I was in the middle of it.

Sexually explicit, disgusting in detail, and everywhere I looked there were bodies that looked like sixteenth century art, body parts that were highlighted so the bodies were slightly deformed and the parts being emphasized were grotesquely exaggerated. I wasn't titillated by any of the scenery or what was going on around me; I was merely aware of its focus and subject matter. It must have been expressing some form of magnified guilt dealing with simply the practice of sex—part of being a single woman.

In that role, I had felt terribly guilty leaving my son for an evening or for a weekend in order to date, especially since I worked so many hours every day with my new business. But since I was desperately trying to find a suitable mate with whom I could rebuild a life for myself and my son, dating was necessary. Every time I was away from my precious child I missed him dreadfully, and felt guilty doing whatever it was I was doing, and frankly, once in a while physical intimacy was involved. I adored my little guy and felt like I was abandoning him for my own selfish interests. I also had a lot of guilt working full-time (actually, more than full-time) but that was survival—not a choice, as dating was. So the guilt relative to dating any man for me was much more intense.

In this dream, with all the bodies and body parts everywhere, I couldn't find my little Jon. He was gone. I ravaged through the throngs of people desperately trying to find my beautiful little boy. He was nowhere to be found. With him missing, my guilt was so intense and the pain so horrible, I can't even begin to describe it. I've never felt anything like it before. I also sensed Jon would be in danger if I didn't locate him soon, and that intensified the panic of my continual search.

As it turned out in the dream, I never found Jon and ended up waking while still feeling all those horrific feelings. The pain in that dream was 1,000 times greater than anything I had ever felt in my life and I wondered how anyone else could survive such emotional trauma.

I woke up exhausted and still in pain. I ran to my meditation room, grabbed my pad and began asking for help with this. I needed to understand. The answer I received was surprising but rang true. I was told that I had just experienced "hell."

That "hell" is the self-punishment we deliver to ourselves in either reliving emotions we experienced in our lives with which we have never effectively dealt, or experiencing the hurt and pain we caused others through our attitude or actions.

In those emotions with which we were to cleanse, our anger, fear and guilt are among the most prevalent. On the other side, if not released adequately here on earth, the primary emotions surface and we experience them to the *nth* degree, living through related experiences that intensify the feeling. This judgment and punishment are self-inflicted and not bestowed on us by anyone or anything else. Once we have satisfied ourselves that we've paid for whatever it is we think we did in our lifetime, we can move on to more comfortable places in the afterlife.

With the pain we caused others, we become aware of those incidences and feel what they felt—magnified by hundreds and hundreds, maybe more.

I also learned that the best way to prevent that type of trauma when we transition is to correct our mistakes as we become aware of them and to be remorseful. Also to prepare better here and now for the feelings we hold onto that are harmful to us. We must learn to forgive ourselves. Forgiveness heals, and we are told God loves us unconditionally and forgives us for everything. So we are the ones who need to be more like Him and have the same charity toward ourselves as we are taught to do with others.

So, alleviating guilt by making amends helps, but alleviating guilt by forgiving oneself may be more powerful. Forgiveness is not only a great lesson to learn, it could be the difference between heaven and hell.

In a message to me from my friend Jack, on December 14, 2011, he confirmed that my dream and perception about hell was "spot-on." When asked about it, Jack said,

"Right on. You got that one early. People so overcome with fear and fear-based emotions experience what you did, then they get to the cleansing place. They don't stay there except for how long they need to be there to rid themselves of all that stored crap. Sometimes it's horribly painful, but the judgment is self-rendered, not by others."

When I asked if I was supposed to communicate this stuff, Jack said at the time,

"Yes, in a blog."

So I did. That's why I thought it was important to share it here as well.

Do You See Any Really Bad Souls Up There?

With the subject of Hell surfacing, the obvious question to Jon, as a follow-up was to ask about the name that first came to mind when thinking of the most evil of people: Hitler. So I asked if those horrible people were in the same place or somewhere else? I was curious about how that all played out on the other side.

"Well, it doesn't quite work that way. No labels here, so no way to know the soul-based struggles others may or may not be experiencing. We kind of hide or are more faint to others while we are going through all that clearing and self-reflection. Like we're invisible. Like we can't and don't interact 'cause we have our own internal issues. It's like if you were printing a color that was five percent intense versus a hundred percent intense. Those of us around here are a hundred percent intense (soul-wise) *pretty quickly, even though our frequencies may vary. But when you are buried in self-reflection, trying to figure out what you did and becoming aware of soul growth needed, you're more faded.*

So, I guess Hitler and a bunch like that know love is out there 'cause they came through it to get here, but are deep in their own crap and the bad ones may take a long time – even for here – to pull away from those experiences. So we don't bump into them because they don't deserve it—missing all the beauty and love and joy and bliss in all forms."

"Real dummies for chasing that life path. Don't know if that was their intent or they chose the wrong fork in the road and bit into that damn apple! Thus shifting their life in a 'possessed' kind of manner. You know how that can happen with psychic attacks and dark and negative energy that's out there too. That's why you clear all the time Momma, and why you and Shirley do work on you periodically."

Jon was referring to how aware I am of shifts in my energy and attitude toward life. When I become more intense, more agitated, more irritable and know that really isn't me, but is generally more about having picked up dark or negative energy somewhere. I immediately clear my energy and then I'm right back to normal. I have friends who ask me to clear them occasionally too, and I can do that remotely. So this entire subject is not some bizarre thing for people who work with energy to understand.

Jon saying that maybe Hitler got possessed at some time in his life either dramatically, over time, or was drawn slowly into a very dark place, is hard to know. But at some point all of us would be wise to take a look at our behavior and say, "Huh?" then course-correct. The exception to people not automatically doing that may be when power and ego are benefited by the negative shift and then the reward for such behavior is just too much to resist. The devil knows what he's doing, doesn't he? The reward for evil behavior can be so intoxicating, some people can't resist continuing with more and more of the same.

Jon went on to say,

> "Did that help? I'm not an expert on that—better go to the source for that question. God will help next time He/She contacts you. No gender here, just energy. ☺"

The Subject of Purgatory

Jon had something important to say about purgatory when I posed the question to him. When I asked if purgatory happened before we get to Heaven, he gave me his perspective:

> No, that's a reflective time. Some of us need more time on that than others. I was pretty advanced, realized I had picked this life intentionally – to learn and grow. Others are sometimes confused because they are part of a 'team' and get recruited to play a role and just nod and say, 'yeah' and get born. Maybe not bright, maybe not paying attention, maybe very young souls, whatever the reason the later groups require more self-reflection time to figure out what they did wrong or right. I knew right away what my role was and what I was to learn, and the minute I got here was glad it was over."

My take on that is Jon had to hurry up and become savvy very quickly so he could help me with this book.

The Subject of Limbo

When I was young the concept of Limbo was very much alive. That was the place, according to centuries of tradition and teaching, where babies who died and had not been baptized went. It took until 2007 for the Church's International Theological Commission said that Limbo reflected an "unduly restrictive view of salvation." But even back in 2005, Pope Benedict expressed doubts about the concept.[8]

After reading this description, no doubt you agree. There again is where I believe religion often oversteps with countless rules, regulations, restrictions, misinterpretations and judgments that are not rooted in the pure love of a compassionate and adoring God. Therefore, Limbo is a non-issue and I only included it to point to the imperfection of many religions, not just Catholicism, as others have their share of off-course judgments as well.

For those devout in a religion, I can seriously understand if they find many elements of this book hard to digest. Hopefully there will still be parts of what Jon or others have shared, or what I've commented on, from this chapter that they can embrace to make their lives easie

Chapter 11

OTHER VOICES, OTHER RELIGIONS

Over the years I've received many, many messages from the other side from voices representing religions that were not Judeo-Christian-oriented. Most of those religions I knew very little about and was surprised that those teachers reached out to me. But since their messages and those I have received from Jesus, Mother Mary and God, Himself, are so consistent regarding love, fear and the concept of connecting with dimensions other than this one, there was no question that they needed to be included.

Each one speaks to the power of love and some to my role in communicating messages from them to you. I never understood the scope or the similarity among different religions on these issues until I dug out a few of those older messages, and again, the dots seem to connect. The first was from Buddha in November of 2007.

> *"My child. I've never come to you before but I am here now to assure you all the Ascended Masters are behind you on this project and where you are to be for the rest of your earthly journey."*

The key phrase is *"the rest of your earthly journey"* since in the remainder of the message he was speaking about the book I was writing at the time, which was published in 2008. That book was inspired as well, and dealt with how, if we desire, we can all be led to the perfect answers to heal our bodies naturally. God always provides the answers and He did so in the extraordinary world He created, with medical physicians being among those options. But the book did not focus on the aspects of helping us heal that conventional medical care does brilliantly: orthopedic surgery, reconstructive surgery, emergency care and immediate care for very acute conditions.

No, that book's focus is on the chronic issues, even those which might be eventually life-threatening, and which conventional medicine designates as incurable once they slap the chronic label on it. That book was based on my own personal journeys, the way I found answers to recover from more than six conditions without pharmaceuticals or anything that would harm the body. I wanted to share what was possible for others, so *Get Well—Even When You've Been Told You Can't* was born. It was a process book, not a prescriptive one so it was written to describe holistic healing in-depth.

Buddha went on to speak in that message about other aspects of my life, the lessons I was to learn, and how my service to others will be fueled by love and will be fun. Finally, he said something bizarre at the time and I never "got it" until now:

"We will help you see your son in a way that relieves your pain."

Again, Jon's and my relationship had been painful for me over the years, even though I adored him. My son did as much as he could to distance himself from me, without being cruel and without a total break. I never would have guessed that would ever change. I was happy with the bits of him I received and didn't expect more. Today, my pain is more than relieved; any pain I've ever had seems irrelevant compared to the joy I feel with this new relationship with my son.

In that earlier message, Buddha went on to say,

"You don't know me, Sandy, but all of us here are in love and light. So are you. Your light will brighten over the next years and through the end of your days here on earth, and you will be a catalyst to rise others up and for them to see and reach their potential."

I guess I started trying to empower others regarding their healing, then it was work I did with helping empower women through a nonprofit in which I was involved. Later, it became young, troubled teens to which my heart reached out to encourage work being done to help them find their voice and self-respect. Now I'm trying to empower others regarding finding a deeper connection to love. Rereading that message was wonderful for me, and wouldn't it be nice if Buddha was actually correct? I didn't have to be a Buddhist for him to pay me a visit. He didn't judge any religious connection—the connection with him was all about love.

Another who connected with me quite a few times is Isis, the Egyptian goddess, who is considered to be an Ascended Master too. Even though many would view her as merely a pagan idol, I do not judge, which is probably why she became fond of me.

Isis was considered the goddess of fertility and motherhood, as well as a female creator. She represented our feminine aspects, creation, birth, intuition, psychic abilities, higher frequency vibrations, love and compassion. I also believe she cared about health and healing as she often spoke to me about those subjects while I was in the midst of my first book. Her initial message came to me in the summer of 2007, and in total, I've heard from her eleven times. Never in a back-and-forth dialogue; but always just advice, support or guidance.

One such communication arrived on Valentine's Day, 2014, and ended with something interesting about my son. Isis said:

> *"Jon is coming back to the Jon we all love. Takes time. Be patient. He adores you, Sandy. Always know that."*

I thought she was referring to Jon in this lifetime and to his recent recovery from his opioid addiction, but I don't think she was. I think she was talking about Jon after his passing.

Then, on June 11, 2014, Isis encouraged me about my future, as I was stressed at the time, just beginning to wrap up my final major healing journey and getting ready to eliminate the last elements of stress in my life. Isis came again and began:

"If you could see the legions of angels, the hoard of guides, the Ascended Masters and all of us here waiting for your rebound. Soon my child, soon. Trust me on this. Then, in a couple years you will write again—prolifically and brilliantly. All will benefit.

"It is not over for you. You will have twenty years left. You will see a great-grandchild and you will watch your son rise from the ashes."

Although this was the second time for a very strange reference to Jon, I didn't put the two comments together since when I receive a message, I rarely go back and re-read old ones and try to make sense of it all. I just receive what's sent to me and move on.

Only in retrospect does any of this truly seem logical now. Her final message came on May 3, 2015 when she said:

"You are a healer—an emotional healer, a physical healer, a spiritual healer. The Bible will be good for you to crank all that up again; and, write, you must. Begin blogging again. Your thought process is profound. You channel Masters and all of us. People need that."

I didn't blog much, since I really didn't understand how to make the blog go anywhere except within the confines of my computer. When I did blog it was on one of my websites. Actually, the one I called my woo-woo site.

The reason I went back to dig up some old voices from the past is that as I was writing this book, I didn't want people to sense any bias toward Christianity. My personal preference has nothing to do with the content of this book—it was to be universal and totally inclusive. I've always been reverent of all religions, and at the same time critical of them all too. Yet, as all those other voices came, they always came of their on volition. I never summoned them, except for this one exception.

Since I had wanted to make sure this book was balanced and that no one who wanted to be involved would be under-represented, I was talking out loud one day about it and said that if anyone else who wasn't included in this book wanted to be a part of it by sharing their perspective on love and connectedness, they can contact me. I was prepared to make a conscious attempt to invite them by asking God for help that evening before I went to bed, hoping in the next day or two someone would respond. I forgot to do that.

Well, throughout the balance of the day a name kept popping into my head: Ram Dass. I'd guess that's because a friend had sent me a beautiful photo with one of his famous quotes on it months before and I had filed it away on my desktop for reference and had intended to include it in this book. I never got around to doing anything with it and I thought the name popping into my consciousness was just because I knew a bit about him. When I say a bit, that may even be an exaggeration.

I knew Ram Dass was some kind of teacher and perhaps was connected with some Eastern religion or philosophy, but really my knowledge didn't extend past that. And when his name came to me, I just ignored it, a couple of times, actually. Then, a couple of days after I spoke out loud about the invitation, my email suddenly stopped and disappeared from my desktop. Gone. I opened it up again and it reacted weirdly once more, which it had never done before since everything else regarding my computer was in perfect working order. *A signal from someone,* I thought. I asked and that was confirmed. So I went to my desk, grabbed a pen and pad and began to write.

> *"Hello Sandy. I am new to you. My name is Ram Dass. My name kept popping into your head yesterday because I was nearby. I have spread the word and I do want to be included in your beautiful book.*
>
> *"Love—yes. Drop fear—yes. Connecting with all of us or any of us—yes. The beauty of life is the unlimited potential it offers through love. If one's heart is pure, intention is in love and soul is determined to grow, nothing is impossible."*

I was shocked and in disbelief but just kept writing. I wasn't sure whether this man was alive or dead, and that uncertainty made me wonder where this message was coming from. I'd never received a telepathic message, that I knew of, and didn't want to start. That was too much of a new arena for me. Anyway, still focused on the message that was being sent, I kept pen to paper.

"We are all created in greatness. That's our destiny. Learn from one another how to become that. Sharing and watching and listening has always been the way. That's how a baby bird flies by learning, absorbing and then spreading its wings to take off. They fly and so can you.

"Baby animals, the same. By mimicking success, you will grow that way as well. People should seek answers from those with more wisdom, and not judge. We should merely see success and wish to emulate. You will teach, my dear Sandy. You will teach by being a conduit for many, many voices. You have love for all. You do not judge.

"Encourage others to open their hearts, to reach above themselves, around themselves and beyond themselves. Wisdom is everywhere and your book helps open those doors.

"In blessings. In peace and forever in love, Ram Dass."

Afterward, I looked him up on Wikipedia and saw he was 88 at that time. It didn't say he was dead, but I did read about him. His real name was Richard Alpert, but he was named Baba Ram Dass by a Hindu named Neem Karoli Baba, a great saint and guru who was also known to his followers as Maharaj-ji.

Ram Dass was an American spiritual teacher, psychologist and author. He was a Hindu. So, thinking he was still alive, I didn't want to put anything in this book that might be even be more questionable, like something telepathic. And since this would have been my first message by that method, I set his message aside; all too weird for me.

A few days later I was on the phone again with my good friend Paige and told her about the weird message and how confused I was about the source since I was sure Ram Dass was still living. She surprised me with her response:

"No, he died in December,"

Paige checked again with her husband while I was still on the phone. Sure enough, Ram Dass had passed. I googled his passing and there it was—he died December 22, 2019. So, this was an actual message and now I had a Hindu voice for my book.

It remains fascinating to me that this final message is so similar regarding love, fear and connecting to all the others. All points of view, from the Buddhist to the pagan to the Hindu, seem to echo the same sentiments as the Judeo-Christian messages I have received. I guess God's voice does permeate all religions.

Chapter 12

EVEN THE MOVIES AND TELEVISION PLAY ROLES

Many people may doubt the existence of an afterlife, the concept of psychic gifts or the mystic in all forms, but they sure enjoy watching stories about them. People have been avid viewers of shows about mediums and psychics, people experiencing Heaven, life on other planets and the world of the unknown for the last fifty years.

I'll bet you can name a number of TV shows or movies that you really enjoyed and didn't judge one way or the other whether they were real or not. I have my favorites. One was the TV series *Medium*, a supernatural drama that focused on the life of Allison DuBois, a housewife and mother with gifts.

Throughout the series, Alison used her psychic visions about dead people in her work as a part-time consultant with the local district attorney's office. Of course, in all of these shows, Allison's gifts were ridiculed and challenged, until at the end when she would always be proven right. Anyway, Patricia Arquette starred in the series and I never missed an episode. I didn't personally relate to any of her gifts, even though my gifts were developing at that time. Perhaps that was because I felt she had more of a natural calling than I. Frankly, even then I minimized everything related to what I was able to do and continued that habit for years. *Medium* ran from 2005 through 2009 on NBC and then for two more seasons on CBS until 2011.[9]

In the last several years the most popular TV series, this one more of a reality show format, is *Long Island Medium*. Not sure if it is still on the air, but Theresa Caputo lives, you guessed it in Long Island, but spends much of her time in the spirit world. She talks to the dead. She is an interesting personality since she doesn't just possess this gift, she thrusts that gift on everyone she meets.

Theresa is aggressively helpful, and the bright light she obviously emits to the other side constantly attracts all sorts of souls who recognize when their loved ones are within earshot of Theresa and that's when the communication begins. Theresa generally conveys short messages but that's really all that most on both sides require. The guy who sells her a pair of shoes, a girl who waits on her table or her unsuspecting gardener are all easy prey. Captive to what she wants to tell them, she ends up bringing closure to many and healing messages to others. It was and maybe still is sort of a cute show, but I'm sure most people don't believe it's real. I do.

The reason I say that I have no doubt about the authenticity of people like Theresa is that for more than three decades I've known that talking to those who have passed is possible. Still, Jon really confirmed how it all happens with his "lights over LA" analogy. Even though I might have been aware of what was real and what was not, to know something is quite separate from understanding how it works. Jon's insights always help me understand or drill down with his answers about methods and process from his perspective.

Some of my friends might believe I have a gift, but might totally disbelieve celebrity psychics who to them are more in show business than in the spirit business. That's probably because so many messages these professional mediums receive are short, simple and common. But those short messages, people like Theresa Caputo share with others may be the only message a loved one who passed needs to convey. "I love you." "I'm okay." Or, "I'm happy." Sometimes the message is conveyed just to let those they love know they are nearby and observing. In the latter instance, these souls may comment on something they saw and appreciated like a graduation ceremony, a family wedding, their house being repainted. Short personal messages meant to prove they're really there, caring and close by.

Famous Psychics and Mediums

Besides the TV medium celebrities, there are also other famous and legendary psychics such as Nostradamus. Legendary Nostradamus was born in 1503 in France and was a clairvoyant whose predictions were well-recorded.

Another legendary figure was Edgar Cayce, born in 1877 in Kentucky. Edgar was a normal child, except for the fact that he could interact with spiritual beings. His notoriety came when he learned he could put himself into a trance and receive information from the other side.

His remedies for healing are still taught today at Association for Research and Enlightenment (A.R.E) clinics worldwide. His readings covered over 10,000 topics and contain 14,306 readings. His prophecies that came true included the 1929 stock market crash, World War II, the shifting of the earth's poles and the ability of medical science to diagnose illnesses with just a drop of blood.[10]

Jeane Dixon was more of a contemporary psychic who was born in 1904 in Wisconsin. She was more like the psychics of today, doing readings for individuals. Other celebrity psychics whose names you would immediately recognize might be Sylvia Browne, who died in 2013, and John Edward, who is also a published author.

Another interesting one is Doreen Virtue. She was previously an angel communication teacher, and an author of many angel oracle card decks and metaphysical books published by Hay House, and has been very successful over several decades. Doreen is a well-educated, New Age voice with both a B.A. and M.A. in Counseling Psychology. And is a very pretty blonde. In 2017 she totally dropped out to pursue an M.A. in Biblical and Theological Studies as a born-again Christian and denounces every aspect of the New Age movement. Sad, really, because one can blend Christianity with God's gifts and clearly angels are one.

I am not and have never been part of the New Age community, and instead have always danced around the fringes of both that world and the world of organized religion. I adopted my own hybrid method of reaching out to God. He reached back and has blessed me in so many ways, even though some might say I've led a challenging life. Yet I believe my life has been fortunate in that all adversity opens doors for a soul to become closer to God. The gifts He has given me have also enriched my life, as it has with any of the individuals I'm describing in this chapter.

Sharing information about some of the more famous mediums and psychics begs the question, did I ever seek one out? Sure, more frequently when I was much younger and without a rudder to guide me. I was still bouncing around among religions, yet to have formulated my own path to God. And uncertainly often opens the door for fear, which is not healthy. So on occasion I'd go see someone, primarily to provide a little hope. That worked until I developed true faith. It was also great entertainment especially when I was dreadfully bored about my life: hearing instead about the next gorgeous, interesting or fascinating man who was about to enter my life. Having a "story" to share was always a fun exercise with girlfriends, and although I doubt that many of us believed much of what was predicted, it certainly gave us something to talk about and a little to look forward to.

There is another category of refined access to the events and people in the past, present and future. Some people are gifted to tap into what is called the Akashic Records. As Deepak Chopra calls it, the Akashic Field. That subject is way too complex to delve into in this book, so I won't even attempt it. If you think psychics and mediums are way out there, this category of viewing is another step beyond.

Everyone knows Deepak Chopra, MD is the legendary and brilliant author who bases much of his teachings on science. He is highly credible. In a recent video on YouTube, he addresses all categories of individuals with gifts. I am paraphrasing from my notes, and he said something like this: Such individuals, through transcendence, can now have refined intuition, insight, paranormal abilities, precognition, the ability to remember other lifetimes, do remote viewing, remote healing and have extrasensory perception. Some individuals have one or the other or multiples of those. These people with dormant non-local potentials, as Chopra refers to them, are merely exercising abilities that exist in every human being. I believe that too. We humans have yet tapped into the enormous potential that lies within each of us. I'm not striving to do that, but it is amazing how God has made some of that possible in my life so that I could perhaps open the door for others to live a fuller and more richly connected life.

I mentioned my friend Shirley earlier in this book. As a former utility senior executive, she hardly fits the role of having "gifts" and at the time she didn't. But over time, for her, gifts have also developed. Shirley is now quite good at hands-on and remote healing, both gifts she developed when she was in her sixties. So, it's never too late.

Back to the subject of psychics, I do have a very good friend who is excellent at describing for me men who are about to pop into my life over the next few months or year. Tammy doesn't specialize in love interests, she is just really good for me at predicting that aspect. So when I've been bored with my personal life in the past, I've called Tammy for a quick read and a smile.

Tammy refers to herself as a psychic medium but she has also consulted with clients on their life issues using her background studying with Marianne Williamson on *The Age of Miracles*. Tammy is one of the better psychics, and a very good medium, but I personally don't need much external help with the medium part anymore and would now not ask her about long-term guidance, as a psychic, since God helps me there. If truth be told, I really don't want the answers in advance. I like the surprises life presents. So instead of asking, I just pray for the daily strength, wisdom and courage to make it through whatever I'm dealt. It's more fun to watch my life's journey unfold on a daily basis. I prefer to enjoy the ride.

Other famous personalities in this sphere are James Van Praagh, another capable medium who has been on television and attracted many individuals to his appearances in smaller venues (2,500 or less). John Edwards is similar with his appearances where his readings are done for members of the audience. In both these cases, their bright light is recognized by the other side and if a soul seeks their loved one nearby, they may jump in with a message.

I have no doubt these celebrity readings are real. Again, but because so many of the messages are simple, observers don't believe them to be authentic. Yet, using simplicity might be the only way the soul on the other side wants to connect, especially in public.

Back to the Movies

Films and TV shows that recount the existence of angels are endless too. Some are classics: *The Green Pastures* (1936); *It's a Wonderful Life* (1946); *Heaven Only Knows* and *The Bishop's Wife* (1947); *Heaven Can Wait* (1978); *All Dogs Go to Heaven* (1989); *Angels in the Outfield* (1994); *Michael* with John Travolta (1996) and *Fallen* (2016). Well, there are so many films that have made their mark; nearly seventy from my first count.

On TV there have been more than fifteen series dealing with the "other side" including *The Twilight Zone*; *Little House on the Prairie*; *Highway to Heaven*; *Touched by an Angel*; and more recently *Miracle Workers* and *Good Omens*, both of which are still on the air. Could be wishful thinking, but I believe people watch these shows because there's a little spark inside each of us that knows angels just might exist. Even a series like *Blue Bloods* has had a couple of shows dealing with a medium with "gifts"—and although this character possessing a gift is initially viewed skeptically, she always ends up being completely accurate.

The movies have made their impact in the world of exploring the afterlife and Heaven, in particular with films such as *After Life* (Japanese film); *Always*; Defending Your Life (a comedy with Meryl Streep); *Dragonfly* (with Kevin Costner); *A Ghost Story*; *Heaven Can Wait*; *Hereafter* (directed by Clint Eastwood); *The Sixth Sense* (with Bruce Willis); *Truly, Madly, Deeply*; *What Dreams May Come* (with Robin Williams) and *Wings of Desire*. These aren't low budget B-films. These are widely accepted films people still watch. The trend today with the most current *Heaven is for Real* film is to confirm the existence of an afterlife by a person who has returned from some type of near-death experience.

A Young Artist's Gift

To me, perhaps an even more powerful story and one to which I seem to relate is the story about the young girl, Akiane Kramarik, who was born into poverty in rural Illinois. Her family had no money, no friends, no relatives, no television or radio, so Akiane wasn't influenced much by the outside world.

With such a simple life, she took long walks in nature with open conversations and hands-on explorations of knowledge. Her mother was a Lithuanian immigrant educator and her father was a chef with a Catholic background. In her early life there was no prayer, no discussions of God and no visits to church, yet in this insular atheistic environment, Akiane began talking about God.

Her colorful dreams and visions about heaven, Jesus and God's amazing love were eventually translated into paintings when she was only four years old. At eight, she decided she wanted to paint the face of Jesus based on the visions she had received.

Ironically, the young man for which the book *Heaven is for Real* was written and later the movie was made, Colton Burpo, identified Akiane's painting of Jesus as the closest representation of the Savior he had witnessed in his dramatic vision.

I think the most important point is that although Akiane was only seventeen in 2012 when this particular article in *God Reports* was written, she states that her spiritual epiphanies caused her parents to start seeking answers about being Christian, being Catholic and about studying Buddhism. The family members have each found his or her path to connectedness, but Akiane's discovery of God remains remarkably personal. She went on to say that she belongs to no denomination or religion; she belongs to God.

Once a person has been touched directly, through an event, over a period of time in growth, or through some type of conversion, it is difficult to shift away from that direct connectedness. Therefore, the power of those incidents and the impact they have, even secondhand on others, inspires books, films and the TV series I have mentioned. All of this isn't hidden under the rug anymore.

Of course, my favorites of all time in the movie genre are the George Burns series: *Oh, God; Oh, God, Book II; Oh, God! You Devil*; as well as other fun classics: *Evan Almighty* (Steve Carell) and *Bruce Almighty* (Jim Carey). Each of these films personalized God in a way that made talking to Him quite natural. If you think about it, these weren't just funny movies about God talking to an earthling, they were about the very possibility of God talking to an earthling. These films, and their amazing commercial appeal, opened up a whole more acceptable perspective about one's potential relationship with God.

Literature has made its own contribution to this phenomenon. Most recently with the Neale Donald Walsch series of nearly fifty books, six of which made *The New York Times* bestseller list and twenty-eight books have been translated into thirty-seven languages. His first book, *Conversations with God: An Uncommon Dialogue, Book 1* started everything. Walsch was called to write and make the book available to others, which he did by self – publishing the first copies. Then, the earlier book was picked up by Putnam (smart move on their part) and in 1995 became an international bestseller, remaining on *The New York Times* Bestseller List for 135 weeks.

Walsch is an interesting guy. He's a year older than I and was born in Milwaukee, Wisconsin. Also raised Catholic, he too went on a quest for spiritual truth in his life. Although he says his books are not channeled, and many may not be, he says they are inspired. That is probably what his publisher preferred.

His first book however is the most pure and, in my opinion, is the same kind of dialogue that I have with the other side, including from time to time with God. In the introduction of the first printing of *Conversations with God*, Walsch explains how his dialogue with God began, and he clearly admits it's a dialogue.

I'm paraphrasing here, but having basically hit bottom with everything life had thrown at him over the last several years, Walsch kept asking God, in writing through journaling, why this was happening to him, why his life was in such a shambles, and why, why, why? In fact, this frustration, or venting as we might call it, lasted quite a long time. Walsch wrote down his questions in ramblings, and eventually began to receive answers.

This first book is quite pure and I have no doubt when you read the responses that God spoke to Walsch, He speaks to many. Walsch may not call this channeling but when you have dialogue across dimensions, ask questions and write down the answers, it is a form of automatic writing, which is channeling. I can't speak to the quality of the balance of his books but if you have not read *Conversations With God: An Uncommon Dialogue, Book 1*, it's a must read.

Religion Passes Judgment

Other books, where the other side was directly involved in the writing, leave a similar impression and impact with readers as the Neale Donald Walsch works. Almost seventy years ago, A.J. Russell published a book titled *God Calling*. Instead of taking credit as the author, the front cover says: Edited by A.J. Russell. This book of daily devotionals has challenged and informed millions of readers around the world.

Years later a book of daily meditations titled *Jesus Calling* written by Sarah Young, was inspired by Russell's earlier work. These books have a purity about them that challenges a person to doubt that God had a hand in both.

Both are books that fundamental religious groups have rallied against in their particular journals. Additionally, the Vatican has condemned the process of "automatic writing" in order to connect with the other side. I think the scope of "automatic writing" is fairly broad, and although I do a form of it, I don't fit the mold as defined in some quarters about how this method of communication works. Regardless, to condemn any direct method for hearing from God is sad and I'm of the mindset that the Church doesn't always get things right.

On a related note, I once visited a Greek Orthodox monastery in Arizona and was taken on a personal tour by one of the priests. When we entered the main body of the temple, where women sit on one side and men on the other, I was asked about my religious beliefs. After I mentioned to the priest that I had practiced Catholicism at one time in my life but now prefer to pray directly to God, the priest responded in a shocked tone:

> "Oh, my. You have to be careful because you have no idea who you are talking to."

I was instantly offended. *What arrogance*, I thought. How could this man lecture me that the only way to speak to God was through a priest, church or some form of organized religion? I wonder if he thought back to when God first touched his heart and gave him this calling before he was ordained. Was that really God who was communicating with him? Of course it was, and here he is now in service. But his reaction to my comment was fear-based and I question how divine the source was that put that thought into his head. Taking this a step further, would it be questionable if a layperson is called into nursing or healthcare or a person is led to helping special needs kids or even if a good soul is guided toward helping the homeless? How would any of those callings be inspired by evil?

Anyway, my experience with that particular Greek Orthodox priest was one example of misplaced judgment, but the Vatican's history of judging is another. The subject of Vatican condemnation has seemingly been irrelevant in the scheme of things recently, and I hope I haven't offended anyone with such a comment about the leadership of the Catholic Church. So let me explain. The Church has made it a policy to ban anything with which it disagrees or that which might be threatening to its traditions and teachings. History documents this fact. Esteemed writers, philosophers and scientists such as Jean-Paul Sartre, Voltaire, Immanuel Kant, John Milton and Galileo all had works banned by the Catholic Church in its famous *Index Librorum Prohibitorum* (*Index of Prohibited Books*) prior to that process being formally abolished by Pope Paul VI in 1966. Over 4,000 works were labeled as damaging to the faith or morals of Catholics, and followers were threatened with excommunication for reading, publishing, selling or even possessing them.[11]

Additionally, movies were also highly targeted in an effort to "purify the cinema," and beginning in 1933 the Catholic Legion of Decency, a Catholic film register wrote reviews and rated films for their followers. Although this process eventually disappeared, some great films were on their list: *From Russia With Love* (1963); *The Good, The Bad And The Ugly* (1966); *A Clockwork Orange* (1971); *Last Tango in Paris* (1972); *Taxi Driver* (1976); *Scarface* (1983); and *Fight Club* (1999), among others.

It's difficult for me to determine whether all this was because they needed to protect an ignorant flock incapable of separating good values from bad, or incapable of realizing a story was fiction rather than fact? Or, was it in an effort to keep people ignorant. Either way, it breaks my heart because of the immense joy one can feel when the hand of God reaches out and actually touches a person with guidance, love and yes, wisdom, thereby allowing one to access gifts He has given us all—without expecting the worse from us in the process.

The Catholic Church has done a fair amount of judging others. I believe that's ironic since their criticism of movies, books and other methods of reaching God that are unhealthy or harmful to others, doesn't track with some of their own behavior over the years. The old saying that those who live in glass houses should not throw stones may apply here.

What is the Underlying Message?

With all of these works—be they books, films or sitcoms or reality TV shows— dealing with a broader spirituality, there's almost always a good underlying message in most of them. The message that God is always loving not punitive, that the higher human values are rewarded while the lower values are discouraged, and that love is always embraced. Finally, that coaching and supporting is forever encouraged, even by God, and that it is more fun with a dash of humor thrown in.

Everyone seems to watch these entertainment programs and feel better afterwards. Jon, in fact, loved *Long Island Medium* and I think he knew that I did something similar, but we never spoke about the details and he never asked me. Of course, since I held much of my activities in that arena close to my vest, I really didn't talk to many about it, except for a handful of highly spiritual friends.

Anyway, as I go back and read through some of the most wonderful of the books I have mentioned, I always feel love. The same with my memory of the films I most adored.

There was especially love behind the humor.

The messages I receive from the other side are always supportive, loving and complete. No ulterior motives, nothing that makes me feel uncomfortable, and nothing that involves other people other than to love and embrace them with more compassion. That's how I know the messages I receive are not from anything evil. There is no manipulation, there is no prodding, there is no judgment or conviction of others, there is nothing that would cause worry or promote fear; and those are all the weapons of what some might call the devil or the evil one.

Everything I have ever received from the other side has been from loving, supportive sources. Even friends and family who have passed have souls with a divine spark and a sweetness about them. You'll see what I mean in the last couple of chapters.

Chapter 13
HAPPY BIRTHDAY JON

his book is my son's fiftieth birthday present. I started it on October 7, 2019 when I returned home from Jon's fiftieth birthday party that a few of his industry friends threw in his memory at a local restaurant. The event was wonderful. Jon's children came and I'd guess thirty to thirty-five of Jon's business associates attended. At that event, they raised several thousand dollars to benefit the educational trust I had established on behalf of Charlie, Jack and Lucy's continuing education. That trust was one way for Jon's memory to stay alive in a very positive way.

But when I arrived home I didn't feel like I had done enough to honor this milestone in my son's life. Even though he wasn't there to share it, it was a milestone nonetheless and the party thrown in his honor reminded me of the fact that I had, three months earlier, turned seventy-five. As always, I could never forget Jon's or my age since there was a twenty-five-year difference between my son and me.

What I could do to honor this particular milestone hit me directly in the face when I returned home. Jon had been nagging me over and over in our conversations about writing a book on connecting dimensions. The first of such messages from Jon came on September 14, 2018, just two and a half months after his passing:

"*You have to get people to understand how close we* (on the other side) *are!*

Somehow, someway. I guess the opportunity will present itself, but that must go on your bucket list."

The next time Jon reminded me was when I was out for an evening walk. I'd walk down 72nd street, on which my house sits. As always, two of the street lamps were dark, or barely illuminated. Well, until I walked under them, that is. Suddenly one or the other of the bulbs would flash on when I was first approaching or when I was directly underneath them – sometimes both. They weren't on a sensor because I'd see others walk under those lamps and nothing would happen. It was always just me. And whenever the lights would come on, I'd ask, "Honey, is that you?" and I'd hear:

"Yes Momma." Or *"Yes Momma, it's me."*

This time it was just a communication while I walked, so I didn't rush home to take notes. It was slow and relaxed and comfortable. Jon talked and I listened. Sometimes I'd ask questions but the overall theme of this particular conversation was the need for me to write a book on this subject.

Jon said I was supposed to tell my story about intuitive development and end with communicating with him and bridging the dimensions. He said people would be interested in how a normal person at forty develops such a gift by accident, and in how I was able to transition spirits, learn to meditate, and segue into channeling all while finding personal guidance that I'd eventually use to help others. He wanted me to share how all these experiences led to my personal and spiritual growth, and how now I am totally at peace, spiritually enlightened and evolved into what he called "a master teacher' just by listening. I'm not sure about that last label, but my son thinks very highly of his mother.

He continued by saying that although I never changed who I was, I grew from these experiences. And he stressed how my story could teach others that it isn't impossible to continue their growth throughout the years, even in this particular arena too. Most importantly, how connecting with our most precious loved ones can be the extraordinary outcome. He mainly wanted me to share how this gift has now given me peace with his passing, and how my philosophy about why we're here and why life happens as it does was reinforced by the additional insight Jon helped me realize. Overall, he said that I am supposed to share in this book everything I've learned.

My initial reaction was to think that the subject matter might be too broad, but Jon didn't see that as an issue. He thought people could simply find the parts that fascinated them the most and learn from those. The moment I returned home, I wrote down the summary of what Jon had said to me on that walk so I could remember and honor his wishes eventually. It was on October 7, 2019, right after I had returned home from Jon's party, that I sat down at my computer to begin.

"Happy Birthday Jon,"

I said out loud as my fingers hit the keyboard and the first chapter title flew out of me in a torrent. The words came rushing forth like someone had just turned on a water faucet at full force. For at least three hours I wrote and wrote and wrote and the organization of the book fell completely into place. It was like this project was divinely inspired. *What a wonderful way to honor my son*, I thought. I could keep my promise to him and I had a feeling this would be a project we could work on together! What a way to turn fifty—to have someone write a book about you, to honor your memory and help so many people in the process.

Jon continued to come to me with comforting messages and to encourage this work. From time to time, I'd make notes and remember to ask him more questions when he'd show up. I'd gain clarification on little details of the afterlife that I thought everyone might be interested in and then I'd ask him about the important elements of his transition that could enlighten others.

Once I started this book, I received this from Jon:

"I'm here and near forever. And, thanks for my best birthday gift ever!! The book. The one thing we'll be able to do together. Finally, huh? A joyous project. Thank you. Loving you for all eternity, JC."

Then, I made it though a couple of chapters before Jon had mentioned it again. This time it was on October 21, 2019, when I was about two weeks into the process.

"Now, the book! I LOVE IT! (I'm yelling.) *Let it be as long as you want. You write so people want to read more. They'll be fascinated and this book could open up two or three more books for you.*

"Say whatever you want about our life. Don't worry about the kids on this one, the message is too important. Make the chapter titles interesting and vague enough that people can't flip to the one reason they bought the book—like the "HOW TO" part!

"You've got this and I'm here to help. Nothing is too sacred; nothing too private. This is the one thing you and I can do together. Our project. A mother and son thing for the world."

I had been so concerned that Charlie, Jack and Lucy would resist the fact that I was writing about their father's life in intimate detail and talking about being a medium or channeling, all of which would be pretty much news to them. I didn't want them to feel like they had to make excuses for their "grammy". But, how compelled I felt to begin and then to write this book overtook those concerns. I know what extraordinary children they are and what a good job their mother has done with them. Most importantly, I know now they realize how much I adored their father. Somehow, in time, even if they were briefly upset with me, I believed they'd eventually understand and forgive. This was a book for the larger good and it was something their father wanted.

Jon got on a roll, once the book was started and I got message after message containing some reference to this writing and the effort at hand. Now, not every author has the benefit of an ongoing critic. I did. On November 5th of 2019, Jon gave me even more feedback:

"I love the direction of the book. Every nuance is right. Every addition is perfect. I am so happy that my life, with the exception of my children, was not wasted. Thank you for letting me help you

with this. We can finally work together on something. Deep in my
heart, I wanted that but you never made any real money ☺"

I could see his smile flash as he finished that particular remark. Jon
was proud of the unlimited potential he had in commercial real estate
and his very early success. Our income ability was totally different. His
industry had remarkable highs and very deep lows. Mine, conversely, was
always steady but my lifestyle over the years was large, I guess you'd say.
This was something that built over time, it didn't just happen, as Jon's
career potential was prone to allow.

It was joyful for Jon to surpass his mother in the "earnings" aspect, at
least periodically, since I think Jon had always seen me as a fairly large figure in his formative years. I was pretty smart and he never got away with
much as a teen, plus I had wide community visibility involving almost all
aspects of my life from the advertising/public relations arena and politics
to the social world as well as in community service. Most of my awards
and public recognition occurred when Jon was in the highly impression-
able years between nine and twenty-nine. Jon had definitely noticed. So,
when he flashed his first half a million dollar check, I couldn't have been
more proud of him. Not because it was a lot of money, but because his
check was way larger than any of mine !!! He beamed, and I guess even
now he hasn't forgotten his superiority.

Throughout the writing of this book, I struggled and struggled with
the title. Even refining the focus eluded me until I began receiving still
more supportive messages from the Heavens.

Divine Guidance

From time to time I've received messages from a variety of spiritual pow-
erhouses. Jesus or Mother Mary, and yes even God, although never all
at the same time. I've heard much less frequently from Mother Mary, in
fact only four times in over thirty years, so hearing from her is always
surprising. This one project definitely brought out the A-Team, and all
at once.

In January of 2020, within a few days of each other, I had three messages right in a row, first from God, then Mother Mary and finally, Jesus—each encouraging me and helping the focus of this book take shape. It's no doubt I'm supposed to write this book and now. If Jon has any doubt about his acceptance in the afterlife, the big dogs have turned out to support our work. I know God takes no offense to Jon's term for Him as well as the Ascended Masters; it's a cute reference, and just to clarify, God truly does have a sense of humor.

I realize this sounds like I talk to the Almighty all the time, but that's not so at all. However, you'd be surprised by how many works are inspired by Him beginning with their inception, and how many people are anointed to do life changing work. From celebrities led into a spiritual calling and criminals who have been reborn and are now saving countless of spiritual lives, to politicians who are leading others in putting God back into society and our world. I suppose what is most fascinating and why I certainly don't feel like this makes me any sort of special person, is the fact that God typically picks very flawed individuals to do His work.

This seems to be a book *everyone* on the other side wants to be written. And, because the information is so inclusive, I bounced around from title to title and from focus to focus. Should this be about connecting dimensions? Should it be about my son's passing and our relationship? Should it be a "how-to" book? Or, should it be about love?

Jon had his own opinion on November 17, 2019 when he said, like he always did:

> *"Hi Momma, I'm here. Good title for a book, huh? Actually, I don't care what you call it. I'm still here for you and I didn't want you to forget that."*

Amazingly, *"Hi Momma, it's me,"* another term Jon used interchangeably when contacting me, by mid-January of 2020 became the working title I settled on. I think Jon was thrilled:

"Do you know how magical this book will be? I watch you receiving inspiration almost every morning about a new chapter (to clarify)—about refinements (to simplify) and about ways to help people understand—simply, this complex but wonderful possibility for everyone. This is more a NIKE thing. Just do it. Gosh, if people tried to understand it all, they'd be overwhelmed. Over here, I can't even understand it all."

Jon's messages have been ongoing and continual, and in them he almost always mentions this project. He is proud of it and proud of me.

In December, however, I heard from the One. It was December 6, 2019 to be exact, and the light in my master bedroom flashed on and off. After inquiring, it was God. He covered a couple of topics that were pressing in my life and then got to this one:

"The book. Ah-ha. Now there's a big one. You know I planted that seed. You know how many I've given you to write? Many books."

And that's right. I have three or four more stuck in my brain, never having the time to get to them. All about personal growth and healing and finding joy.

He continued, about this book and my concern about a timeline:

"Again, you have time. It doesn't matter if you are slow or stuck one week, you'll fly through the next. Be patient with yourself and the way I am controlling the flow.

"You must take time for gratitude, time for praise and worship. Time to share love. Life is not all work and production Rest, my child, in my arms. Feel my love and sigh in complete contentment."

I did feel pressure to push and to finish but I was tired and other demands in my life were pressing. God knew that and wanted me to relax, and so He continued:

"The focus of the book, I know, is the real challenge for you because you have so much information to share. And, it all is needed and interesting; in fact, fascinating. Listen to Jon. Teach others that what you have with him is possible for everyone. Inspire them and give them hope. Don't overwhelm them with detail. Get out of the branches and see the forest."

"Show everyone how they can turn tragedy in their lives into a gift somehow. In Jon's case, it was my gift to him: perfect timing, which he was lacking this time around. Now look. He will be immortalized. He will help thousands and he can now be the son to you his soul always yearned to be. One you were proud of, one who was always there, the perfect loving son. Now he is!!!"

When I read this last part, I broke down sobbing. I know Jon wanted me to always be proud of him. Yet, he couldn't get out of his own way, and he knew that. He wasn't proud of himself and that was devastating to him. To hear God address the longing of Jon's soul, which rang so true to me, broke my heart. But again, the relationship that I now have with my son is perfection. I see Jon's divinity. I see his love. I know who his soul is; it's the one I first recognized when he was lying in that delivery room staring right at me. That magical little boy who is now a magical soul in Heaven, watching over me, his children and others he adores. Now he is helping me make a contribution and helping those who are open to this kind of growth. This book is his too.

On December 6, just a few days later, my television switched off and on. Again, a message from over there, this time from Mother Mary. She has only come to me a couple of times before in three decades, so I was shocked:

"I'm sorry, I know you are tired but I needed to reinforce just a couple things."

Because her message is so profound I wanted to share it in its entirety:

"A mother's love is the strongest. We go through such pain to bring our children into the world, or many do. We take most of the responsibility for them their entire lives, even as they age, they are always our children. Many die for them, in childbirth—or would run into a burning building to save their babies. No mother ever loses that, even when her child dies first. And that is what keeps her strong. That love, and she doesn't realize that the strength of that love, is the umbilical cord that still binds the two of them after death."

The gentle tone of her words can't come through in transcription, but I felt that tone and the peace it gave me as I took down each word. Then, as I read back the information for deeper understanding, I could feel her love and compassion flow through each word to me and for everyone.

"As with any deep love, friendship or romantic, the thread of connectedness is always there, it remains. You had with Jon even what I did not, until my son returned, and then I knew this was forever. You knew that the moment you heard your boy cry out to you.

"How blessed you are. Don't minimize that gift. Beautify it and let it inspire others to perfect their love in all ways, not just learn to meditate. I hope you know what I am saying."

And I did, for I have always minimized what I've learned, the gifts I have and the knowledge I feel compelled to share with others. I brush everything off as anything but mysterious and as something simple that anyone can do. Even though that is true, in fact, there are so many elements that need to be in place for the gifts to spring forth. Mary went on to say:

"Treasure this gift. You are here to use it for good, to spread the enormous amount of love you have to give. Don't wait for or waste it on one man. Give it to the world. We, here, will love you

10x over what you could possibly receive in a one-on-one romantic relationship."

It had concerned me that I might eventually die alone, not having that one special man in my life to be with me at the end. Mary pretty much blew that concern right out of the water. And, I am very lucky to have many men friends in my life; men I adore and who like me. These are all uncomplicated, platonic relationships between bright, caring individuals who share their wisdom, laughter and insight with one another. Can't ask for more than that, I guess.

Mary finished with:

"Cherish Jack, Charlie and Lucy. They are perfect. They will learn how to love through you. They will learn true joy, true love and the true path of life. And, if you keep the book focused on love, no one can ever criticize it."

Finally, I heard from Jesus—or Jeshua, as I often refer to him. The name Jesus was derived from the Greek form of the Hebrew name Yeshua, sometimes spelled Jeshua.[12] As I mentioned earlier, I pray every morning to be guided to do His will and I ask for Jesus's help along with that from the Holy Spirit. This was His message:

"My dear Sandy. Thank you for all you are doing to follow My will to spread love and to teach everyone how to live a happier, more joyful life on earth and to better prepare their souls for the rest of eternity. Eternity is a long time and these lifetimes are just a flicker of time in comparison. Yet this is when it is easiest to perfect our souls, when having a lifetime experience. Yet, people don't seem to know what to do.

"The Bible is full of stories about believing, having faith, trusting, caring for your neighbor, honoring our parents and fulfilling the commandments Moses brought down from the mountain. They (religious scholars and teachers) preach on my lessons of

existence with stories and more stories but people are slow to learn.

"Life is so simple. Look to God. Open your heart and receive the abundant love until it overflows !! Regardless of your wealth, or stature of the circumstances of your life, none of that matters. Once you feel Divine love, your life changes. But souls seem to believe what they hear and see, not what they know or remember from someplace else.

"Love. The great connector. The great healer. The great peace-maker and the one place where everyone can find warmth and contentment. Your book will help. So glad you changed (or rather) *shifted the focus. Love. You know my dear sister, you feel the love."*

Jesus always referred to me as his sister. As we are all children of God—even He, when He lived on this earth. And He reminded me of a recent guided meditation I had done with my friend Paige, whereby, as I sat in a peaceful place, someone or something would come to me with a gift. I always waited to see who would be coming and what they would bring; it was always some very important message. This time, as I sat on the cement bench in the glorious garden, from far away I could see my son Jon approaching. Behind him, everyone I had ever known or loved, who had passed to the other side, followed behind. It was a cast of hundreds. The message was simple and they all said it simultaneously.

"I love you."

That was their complete message. What joy it brought. Jesus finished with:

"Please know how much support you have from us, Sandy. 24/7. Total support and love. Forever. But, especially on this journey of yours. This was a tough one (my lifetime) *but look at how great you've done. And, look at the extraordinary work that still lies ahead of you. Good thing you love productivity, right?"*

Jesus knows how many books lie in wait. So much to share and so much that will help others.

"That's all I came to say. Just to join the chorus of support for you and your efforts and your splendid intention."

He closed by sharing that I'd never be alone and to sleep well knowing with each new day comes a myriad of opportunities for me to do His work, to help mankind and to bring myself much joy in the process. How blessed I am and how grateful I am for the opportunity to bring this book to all of you.

Thank you, dear Jon, for your wisdom and insight and for inspiring all of us to help others achieve what you and I have. To bring through this book, first, the recognition that our loved ones are close, not far or gone. Second, to acknowledge the signals that periodically come; for they're real. Third, to say to each other now across the dimensions what we always longed to say to each other out loud—how much we love and cherish them. And finally, to open our hearts to the love from those who left us and from the Divine beings embracing us from afar so that we become so filled with unconditional love that it spills onto all humanity. Love is the great blessing.

Chapter 14
UNDYING LOVE

ecently, on March 16, 2020, Jon came to me. Now I'm a little smarter; I'm typing the messages because they are generally pretty long and my hand gets so tired. He doesn't seem to mind. On this particular day, Jon talked about the work he is doing on his soul and how important this connection with me is to him. The reason I'm sharing this is because many of you have a loved one who has passed who is so very sorry for any wrongs they may have caused. There is no doubt of that, for that is what soul clearing is all about. This is how Jon expressed it to me and then he ended the message by saying something very profound, but that is never unusual for him.

"I'm doing okay up here. Been looking at my soul, my life, my intentions and studying the reactions of others in the life I just lived, so I could see how my actions really hurt others. Everything with you is painful for me to watch. That is why this relationship with you now is the most important thing I am doing up here. I'm hoping to heal you and me by being the 'son of your dreams,' helping you, really helping you for once and allowing you to feel my undying love. Now, isn't that a great word? Undying?

"That's exactly what true love is. Well, actually any form of love is undying. It goes on forever. And the power of that ... people (on earth) cannot possibly grasp.

"Just look at nature, Momma. Look closely at the trees and the sky and lush bushes, fields of grass or grain and meticulously chiseled mountains—all masterpieces of God. He created all that

beauty with his amazing love. It's like when we were all eating potato pancakes at your house that one time and I commented that I use your recipe but mine never taste as good. Then, Charlie piped up, he was how old? Ten or so? And said, 'But, Dad, Grammy makes them with love.' So profound and he didn't even know it. Maybe someday it will come out in his writing.

    "So, the power of God's love is shockingly aware to people, the beauty of it, the exceptional-ism of it, even if they don't know that love is at the core of each creation. It is love that smacks them in the face; they notice the details of the beauty a second later."

Love is such a magnificent concept to explore, intellectually, emotionally and physically. The most awe-inspiring concept of exercising love is how God loves and protects us. Even when we see life's tragedies before us, we have no idea what God is doing behind the scenes to manipulate the future so that somehow things come out the way they are intended to.

Releasing Judgment

It's like the story Philip Seymour Hoffman's character in *Charlie Wilson's War* told about the fourteen year old boy somewhere in a distant village. The boy had been given a horse and all the villagers said how wonderful that was. The Zen master said,

    "We'll see."

Then, the boy fell off the horse and broke his leg in multiple places. The villagers thought how horrible that was, but the Zen master said,

    "We'll see."

Not long after a war broke out and all the boys in the village were called to serve, except for the boy with the messed-up leg. At this point the villagers again cried out:

"How wonderful,"

The Zen master said …

Only in retrospect can we know the result of any experience—if it's good or bad. And even then we might not understand the complexity of how that particular event affected the lives of others who might be have been remotely touched. It's smart not to judge, even when the incident is horrific.

God's Love Protects the Victims

In 2012 a tragedy struck in Paradise Valley, Arizona, the affluent part of Metro – Phoenix that weaves geographically into parts of Scottsdale and Phoenix. This idyllic area is nestled in and around the beautiful Camelback Mountain, Mummy Mountain and the mountains around Piestewa Peak that are scattered through Arizona's most populated center.

In that year, a local couple was found dead in a burning home in beautiful Paradise Valley. He was a prominent gastroenterologist and she was a socialite involved with the National Kidney Foundation of Arizona and Phoenix Symphony, among other local charities. I knew Larry and Glenna only casually, but a man I had been dating a year or so prior was their closest friend. My friend, Jack, had started the Food Network a number of years prior, and while we were dating the four of us had dinner together a couple of times.

When the entire community read about the news of the murder in the paper or heard about it on the news, people were stunned. How could such a horrible thing happen? Jack was devastated. By that time Jack had gotten married, so thankfully he had someone to lean on through his grief.

When one of the typical "lights flashing" incidents occurred at my home, I settled in to see who was contacting me and to receive whatever they wanted to say. It was Glenna. At first I was really surprised; I knew her, but not that well. Then, as the message started, it was clear that she wanted me to do her a favor and deliver the message to Jack so he could find peace with the incident.

I'll just give you a few parts of that message to reinforce how souls find whom to communicate with down here, to highlight how souls gain perspective after passing and to show how they are embraced by love once they arrive in Heaven. Hopefully these comments will also illustrate the extraordinary love God has for us and how ridiculous it is to blame God for the choices man makes (free choice, remember?). God just tries to clean up our messes and tries to make the best out of horrific situations. Glenna said to me:

> *"Sandy, I know you have been thinking of Larry and me and how worried and saddened* (all are) *by all of this. I am so happy that I found someone I know to contact now. I am so happy you do this work and had no idea how valuable this is, and if I was there I would spread the word."*

She went on to state that now that the shock of all the horrible events have finally subsided for them, she'd like Jack to know they are both okay now. She went on to describe the man who attacked them as "wild-eyed and obviously on some strong, strong drugs," some of the details surrounding their death, and how badly she feels for her children and friends to have endured this pain too. She continued:

> *"Somehow Larry and I managed to get up here together and the warmth, the peace, the love were so instantly healing. We are now at peace and are able to do the soul work that all of us do on this side.*
>
> *"God is glorious and truly protects victims like us. For some reason the pain isn't really felt before we find we're gone. It's like our brain dopes us somehow to get through it all. Please let others know the suffering was not as horrific as one would imagine and when I was shot I went quickly. Although Larry lasted longer, he was unconscious so you see God did take care of both of us."*

"We feel no hate or animosity for the man who did this. It was what was to be. But he should suffer the earthly consequences of such an act, at least to discourage others and send a message.

"Sandy, I thank you for being there so I could tell someone."

"If he (Jack) is willing to accept any of this, I hope you will let him know or send this off to him. Thank you again Sandy. With love and best wishes for more of this good work, Glenna."

It was a little touchy letting Jack know that I even did this sort of thing, since that wasn't anything I'd shared while we were dating, but he was more than willing to read Glenna's message and asked that I mail it off to him. After receiving it, he called to say that both he and his wife were much more at peace and that the "voice" of the note sounded exactly like Glenna. She had a formal edge to her so even her most candid comments had a professional or buttoned-up feeling about them. Glenna's class was evident throughout her message. Jack was most grateful and I was honored to help.

So you see, what everyone assumed wasn't exactly so.

Understanding Love Versus Fear

The lesson I believe for all of us in this life is that love is what's important. I'm not sure why this simple truth seems to elude folks, but when we understand that there are really only two basic emotions —love and fear—it becomes easier. Yes, the opposite of love is not hate, it's fear. Life seems to shift more into perspective. Let me put that all in context.

All fear-based emotions are negative, harmful and make our lives much more stressful and complicated. Plus, they actually weaken the immune system. I'm allowed to draw that conclusion because of my decades of living with, fighting and conquering a host of autoimmune diseases. Through all that, I gained a certain amount of expertise about dealing with stress and healing, and what it takes for immune systems to recover.

Those fear-based emotions never connect us to wonderful people who will enrich our lives (regardless of the dimension in which they reside), but quite the opposite. In fact, fear-based emotions actually distance us from others. All of those negative emotions stem from fear and you will likely be amazed by how many there are. That's why they are broken into subsets with related feelings following the basic categories.

Grief, is the first—the aversion to accept what is, which is what many feel when a loved one passes. That feeling leads to depression, remorse, despair, gloom, hopelessness, disappointment, suffering, insecurity and doubt.

Apathy, which is a lack of concern or respect for others, is an odd one. Although that feels initially like a neutral emotion, it is not for it fuels hatred, contempt, scorn, indifference, disdain, disrespect, hostility, animosity, loathing and resentment. That makes perfect sense since if you have no respect for others, the door is open to a host of negative and hateful feelings.

Uncertainty, which also might feel like a neutral feeling, is fearing the unknown opening the door to wariness, dread, distress, apprehension, worry, anxiety, doubt, uneasiness and stress. See how this works?

Add to those, shame, which is a lack of confidence and which creates dishonesty, embarrassment, envy, jealousy, disrespect, guilt and humiliation.

Then there is abandonment, the fear of being ignored or forsaken, bringing on feelings of isolation, loneliness, alienation, neglect and desertion.

Horror, the fear of pain, harm, impending doom or imminent death also creates terror, hysteria, shock, panic, helplessness, alarm, fright and disbelief in the hearts of those who feel that emotion.

Finally the obvious, anger. That one word seems like a pure emotion unto itself but it is more complex than that. Anger emanates from fear of the unknown, from passing judgment, or from when we feel wronged, cheated or denied what is rightfully ours. The result is rage, frustration, competitiveness, resentment, bitterness, aggravation and aggression.

Exhausting list, isn't it? Living continually with any of those feelings cannot possibly bring joy, connectedness or feelings that result in security and happiness. Every one of those is fear-based yet it is easy to slip into any one of them throughout our normal routine.

Now let's take a look at the love-based emotions, which present a totally different story. When reading through this list you will see how these feelings bind us to one another, promote warm, wonderful feelings among souls and give us peace. Again, sometimes it's a challenge to see the immediate connection to the initial emotion, but when we read on to the entire list it all makes perfect sense.

Happiness is letting go of all expectations and welcoming the unknown. This amazing feeling opens the window to joy, delight, ecstasy, euphoria, pleasure and bliss.

Empathy identifies ourselves in others, produces compassion, pity, sympathy, kindness and affection.

Certainty, which is a willingness to accept what comes and a belief that all will work out, allows for excitement, relaxation, tranquility, equanimity, faith, self-control and inner fortitude to surface.

Honor—unshakable integrity—is by itself sometimes difficult to describe, but in context of what it creates in a person, the word becomes instantly and totally understood. The by-products are honesty, confidence, resolve, respect, trust, humility and forgiveness.

Belonging, or feeling part of a group, is the precursor to togetherness, support, helpfulness, caring, connection, contribution and dependability.

Wonder, which is gratitude for what life presents, offers as a result surprise, amazement, astonishment and awe.

Lastly, acceptance. The calming and inspiring feeling that produces relief, comfort, non-judgment, cooperation, contentment, and finally, complete peace of mind.

What an amazing way to live—in all the love-based emotions. I wish I could have organized this brilliantly categorized list, but alas I did not. It was compiled from an article at skilledatlife.com and when I first found it I shared it with people who attend my workshops, and now with you. I give the author, although an author was never identified, full credit for the compilation and for making it easy for me to paraphrase what living a life based in love looks like as opposed to living one from a basis of fear.

Love as a Constant in Our Lives

We are each at our best as clear vessels through which God's love flows continually.

When we remain clear, we are also free to receive; reminiscent actually of the old Drano commercials with the transparent pipe through which the full force of fresh, clear water flows. Think of that as our soul on earth. The more we can learn to live with love flowing through us, the more chance it will have to overflow on everyone we know and everyone we touch.

Love is so pure and positive and powerful. It's the great connector. The energy of love is the most powerful in the world. Love is what we always hope to be behind our most well-intentioned prayer, behind nurturing and guiding our children and grandchildren, and the intimate way we touch others we care about in our lives.

When we find ourselves slipping into fear, it's tough to jump directly to love. However, we can connect to love through exercising one of two glorious subset emotions: gratitude or forgiveness.

When we begin to look around us with gratitude, something changes. When we pause and also try to forgive, something also shifts. A sense of humor helps us recover too. Life is truly so very simple, but if we allow love to become more prominent in our lives and therefore shape everything we do, we will go through life with an open heart, become naturally of service to others, feel more compassionate and listen more earnestly.

It also helps to believe in God or something wondrous that is much greater than ourselves. One cannot look out at nature or the creatures that inhabit the great outdoors without seeing beauty, creativity and magic. Once we can acknowledge that such magnificence exists but can't really explain how, we are more likely to accept the concept of a God, and then of a God's love.

A side note: I didn't know where to put this in the book, so it's going here. I wanted to point out something I don't quite understand; the aversion some people have to acknowledge God. I hear "The Universe will bring this to me." Or "I'm connecting with Source." But I don't quite as often hear "God will bring this to me." Or "I'm connecting with God." So, if you prefer the distinction of Universe and Source as your major reference points, I'd like you to consider another perspective. Who do you think created the Universe? The Universe is the delivery system, but there had to be something behind that. The Universe isn't the creator, it is the vehicle.

Well, to some the creator could be the Source. I suppose that works, but Source in description doesn't seem like a loving entity to me. Source sounds institutional, remote, disconnected and impersonal. Whereby God is really a parallel entity by reference and yet instantly sounds more intimate, loving, gentle and kind. By the way, referencing God does not mean you are tied to a religion or endorsing the concept of religion. God came way before any of those. So for me, I'd much prefer pure love and God anytime. Smile.

Love and Frequency

Growing in love helps all of us raise our vibration or frequency. Perhaps that is what Buddhists attempt when trying to reach Nirvana by putting themselves into a state in which there is perfect happiness, an idyllic place. The way I would interpret that is to try to find oneness with God by finding the state of pure love, since that is what God is. Hindus do something similar with their meditation practices to find the perfect state of self, called moksha. Ironically, one doesn't have to fall into some type of trance or state if one can just keep living in the moment, spending every minute with a grateful heart and letting love flow through themselves as we were intended to do. We've just gotten way off track in life. One can be productive, busy and alive, and be fully in love too.

I hope no one thinks I am oversimplifying here, and I certainly hope no one thinks I am minimizing the sacredness of those Buddhist or Hindu rituals. I'm just trying to bring all this down to a very simple, practical and accessible reality for normal people. I feel blessed that God has allowed me to find within my very simple, normal life the most ideal life in the world for me. That is one where I never feel alone, bask in love all day and am able to share that feeling with those for whom I care. Being connected to all the souls beyond is amazing, and Jon, my son, is the frosting on the cake. Our frequency simply grows naturally through very simple practices that don't take months of fasting or other elaborate sacrifices. In fact, the benefits of appreciating love and being open to all related gifts are endless.

If I was ever in doubt that love surrounds us all, I just have to listen to the messages from our families and loved ones who are always there to help comfort and reassure us. How can we ever feel alone with messages like these?

> *"Now, I will spend the rest of your life, loving you every day, every minute and every second from up here. Know I am here for you and I'll see you tonight on your walk. Your loving son, forever and ever and ever. JC"* 4-16-19

> *"I'm here. I'm always here for you. Don't ever doubt it, don't eveworry. Always by your side. Always your son."* 10-1-19

Jon understood the importance of educating people that our friends and families are close, to help mitigate the sorrow and grief people feel upon a loved one's passing and to bring them hope. He knows the value of this connection in his relationship with me, and eventually with others. I also think he is sad at how walled-off people are to receiving love from everywhere !!!

On November, 18, 2019, Jon sent me this in one of his messages. Pretty much sums up everything:

> *"I miss you too. But really we are closer than ever before, every minute of every day. I'm here to comfort you and send love, just like we all are. So tragic that most people are closed off to all this, or don't have confidence in what they see or hear.*
> *"We're always there."*

Love is Always the Answer

The following is from a blog post I was compelled to write on April 20, 2012. This seemed like the perfect way to conclude even though this was years before Jon's passing. Funny how we believe our life is tragic or stressful or painful, when in retrospect little compares to losing the one person you love most in the world. Still, the answers I received from God at that earlier time in my life can help us all:

"When we're in the depths of despair, feel lost, are searching for answers and cry out for help—whatever we ask for or say at the time is generally heartfelt and is heard. Such as it was for me not long ago. Faced with so many variables in my life and none clearly defined in terms of my health, my living environment, my work and the possibility of a romantic relationship lying ahead; all were weighing heavily on me. I guess the reason for the confusion is the timing of all of it: if I did one thing first, it affected the others, etc.

I was even questioning whether all my intuitive work was a conflict with my commitment to my relationship to God, since I had also been allowing Christian teachings into my life once again, which were very comforting. I realized that even though I didn't see a conflict between the two, there might be one. Frankly, I was overanalyzing and trying to control everything that I was completely frozen. Everywhere I looked I saw one issue after another—all unresolved. Meanwhile, money was running out while I struggled with all the uncertainty in my life. There were too many options and no clear direction.

I woke up one morning sobbing and asking God for help to guide me. To direct me and to bring clarity to all the issues I was facing. This is the message I received and the reason I am sharing it is because it's so beautiful. I knew it would help others facing similar challenges. I asked for direction and guidance. This was the message God sent:

"Everyone's job is to bring love. That is who I am and that is what you are meant to express through your relationships, your work and your actions. Don't isolate yourself. Don't hide. That is fear. Love heals—know that.

"In terms of connecting with the beyond, fine, but do so with love. In terms of what medicines to take, who cares? But do it with love. In terms of your own vessel's clarity (eliminating stored negative emotions) and your ability to maintain a healthy body—live only in love. Bathe your soul in love and release anything negative, dark or fearful. You'll be fine and beautiful.

"Love everything. Love your sickness—it gives you time to reflect. Love your poverty—it eliminates stress and helps you simplify life. Love your enemies—they are there to teach you. And, love Me—I am there to guide and protect you.

"In terms of accessing those on the other side, I created angels and all of you, your guides, Ascended Masters and all of everything. So why should you shun away from any of My creations?

"Just remember, love is simple, love is uncomplicated, love is peaceful, love is kind, and love is helpful and trusting. Can you imagine a world filled with that?

"And, regarding Mother Earth. She is Mine too. Love is what she responds to best but she is as complex and sturdy and as resilient as that magnificent body I gave you, so it takes an awful lot to hurt her. Don't fall victim to fear or listen to those who play on fear regarding her. Love her. Love Me.

"Now, for your work. My child, love—and it will come. Love and forgive. It will come in time.

"I haven't abandoned you, it is just your timetable we are working from up here and you have high expectations for yourself. You minimized your future pain. You maximized your strength. We are all trying to help you get through it all easily. Fallback position: love. And, you will love your work. You will love your final home and you will romantically love again. All soon. All soon.

"Now, my child, have peace today. Work on your website or whatever you have planned. It is okay, but always do so with love. Teach love. Live love.

"So, in love, I am here for you —forever."

If you are similarly struggling in your life and confused, disillusioned and even despondent, have hope. God is there for you too. Even if you have lost someone you love, love that loss too, for it isn't really loss at all. It's an opportunity to make the relationship perfect and pure in love. Look *all* around you. Find love, embrace love and give love to one another, for all eternity.

ENDNOTES

1   Pursey, Kirstie, and Kirstie Pursey. "Everything Is Energy and Science Has Proved It – Here Is How." *Learning Mind,* 29 Aug. 2020, www.learning-mind.com/everything-is-energy/.

2   *Monitor on Psychology,* American Psychological Association, www.apa.org/monitor/2019/01/numbers.

3   Howard, Jacqueline. "The US Suicide Rate Is up 33% since 1999." *CNN,* Cable News Network, 21 June 2019, www.cnn.com/2019/06/20/health/suicide-rates-nchs-study/index.html.

4   Daniari, Serena, and Evann Normandin. "Alcoholics Anonymous a Religion? – Rewire.News – Religion Dispatches." *Rewire News,* rewire.news/religion-dispatches/2018/05/18/alcoholics-anonymous-religion/.

5   "Reincarnation." *Wikipedia,* Wikimedia Foundation, 1 Sept. 2020, en.wikipedia.org/wiki/Reincarnation.

6   "Gilgul." *Wikipedia,* Wikimedia Foundation, 10 June 2020, en.wikipedia.org/wiki/Gilgul.

7   "Essenes." *Wikipedia,* Wikimedia Foundation, 14 Aug. 2020, en.wikipedia.org/wiki/Essenes.

8   Pullella, Philip. "Catholic Church Buries Limbo after Centuries." *Reuters,* Thomson Reuters, 20 Apr. 2007, www.reuters.com/article/us-pope-limbo/catholic-church-buries-limbo-after-centuries-idUSL2028721620070420.

9   Medium (TV Series).â€Â Wikipedia, Wikimedia Foundation, 31 Aug. 2020, en.wikipedia.org/wiki/Medium_(TV_series).

10   "Edgar Cayce." *Wikipedia,* Wikimedia Foundation, 10 Aug. 2020, en.wikipedia.org/wiki/Edgar_Cayce.

11 Schlumpf, Heidi. "Does the Church Still Ban Books?" *U.S. Catholic Magazine – Faith in Real Life*, 23 June 2020, uscatholic.org/articles/201009/does-the-church-still-ban-books/.

12 "Jesus." *Wikipedia*, Wikimedia Foundation, 31 Aug. 2020, en.wikipedia.org/wiki/Jesus.

ACKNOWLEDGEMENTS

I wish to thank everyone with whom I connected throughout the writing, publishing and promotion of this book. This was an inspired and talented team. Of course, there are others who I must thank individually, so in no particular order they are:

Rose Winters, CEO of The Foundation for Living Medicine, for introducing me to the team at Waterside Productions as well as for other doors she has opened. She's a catalyst and connector.

Shirley Richard, my dearest friend, for her work with me over the years. Someday she'll recognize what an amazing healer she is. This last time, she saved my life.

Paige Jackson, talented beyond her own awareness, whose work with me stimulated my insight and helped me break through barriers. She's so very gifted.

Dave Alexander, managing member of Caljet of America, LLC and many other companies, for being a dedicated, long-term friend and whose support for his "sister" can't be measured. I'm eternally grateful.

Blessings to all of you for helping me deliver God's work and for making it possible for me to honor my son in such a significant way.

For more information or to contact me personally, please visit my website: www.sandycowen.com.

Made in the USA
Monee, IL
10 May 2021